BARNES & NOBLE FOCUS BOOKS

Barnes & Noble Focus Books on Shakespeare's plays are prepared under the editorship of J. Wilson Mc-Cutchan, Professor of English, University of Waterloo

OTHELLO

An Outline-Guide

to the Play

PAUL A. JORGENSEN, PH.D.

Professor of English
University of California
Los Angeles

NEW   YORK

BARNES & NOBLE, INC.

PUBLISHERS • BOOKSELLERS • SINCE 1873

This is an original Focus Book (Number 703). It was written by a distinguished educator, carefully edited, and produced in accordance with the highest standards of publishing. The text was set on the Linotype in Old Style, Caledonia, and Electra by Hamilton Printing Company (Rensselaer, N.Y.). The paper for this edition was manufactured by S. D. Warren Company (Boston, Mass.) and supplied by Canfield Paper Company (New York, N.Y.). This edition was printed by Hamilton Printing Company (Rensselaer, N.Y.) and bound by Sendor Bindery (New York, N.Y.). The cover was designed by Rod Lopez-Fabrega.

TABLE OF CONTENTS

ACKNOWLEDGMENTS

For my analysis and interpretation of *Othello* I have depended, more than I can acknowledge in occasional footnotes, upon the writings of many scholars. I take this opportunity to thank only a few of those to whom I am most indebted: Lily B. Campbell, Robert B. Heilman, Irving Ribner, Marvin Rosenberg, and Arthur Colby Sprague.

An even greater indebtedness I gladly acknowledge to my Shakespeare students. They have provided me with insights, unsettling questions, and faith in the wide and permanent appeal of Shakespeare. Particularly I am indebted, for expert research and assistance, to Carol Bloom and Joan L. Zachary, who have most materially helped me to see this project through to completion.

I owe special thanks to the General Editor of this series, Professor J. Wilson McCutchan. Without his exemplary book on *Macbeth* and his constant advice and encouragement, I should have found the going very hard indeed.

PART ONE: INTRODUCTION

1. The Tragedy of *Othello*, the Moor of Venice

Of Shakespeare's four major tragedies (*Hamlet, Othello, King Lear*, and *Macbeth*), *Othello* is perhaps the most powerful in its emotional impact. It is, for one thing, compact and intense in its construction. There is also a remarkable concentration upon one person and one emotion. Some emotion is expended upon Desdemona, a little upon Cassio, and an enormous amount of hatred upon Iago, but there is relatively little dispersal of sympathy. What we feel at the end of the play is "the pity of it" (IV,i, 206),[1] and the pity is overwhelmingly for the man who has just murdered his innocent wife. There is a terrible irony, pathetic in the extreme, in the story of a man ignorantly killing, for the sake of "justice," the one person whom he loves most dearly and who has come to be all that gives purpose to his life and separates him from chaos.

Students of the play will wish to examine Shakespeare's means of achieving this power in comparison with the Italian story from which he took the plot and many of the characters. A summary of the Italian story is provided in Part II, Chapter 2. It will be particularly noticeable that Shakespeare ennobles the character of his hero and also tightens up the construction, particularly of that important part, the catastrophe.

Shakespeare's play is also especially gripping because it deals with jealousy, one of the most painful of emotions. It is painful because it is ambivalent—made up principally of two warring elements, love and hatred. This subject will be discussed more fully later (Part II, Chapter 3).

Another important reason for the pronounced and lasting appeal of *Othello* is the question it raises as to why so terrible, and apparently undeserved, a calamity should befall a man like Othello. Some critics, as the reader may see from the selections in Part II, Chapter 6, find Othello not at all blameless. Such critics are not, as a result, emotionally prepared (or equipped) to feel "the pity of it." Most

---

[1] All act, scene, and line references in this volume are to *The Complete Works of Shakespeare*, ed. George Lyman Kittredge (New York: Ginn & Co., 1936).

critics, however, have put the blame for the tragedy upon the re-markable conjunction of a noble and innocent hero and perhaps the most gifted villain in literature. This latter view acknowledges the presence and fateful power of external evil.

The concept of external evil may be criticized as a superficial view of tragedy. Most great tragedy of the Renaissance confronts the pro-tagonist with a moral choice. What he chooses is a result of what he is. Othello, according to the "internal evil" school of critics, would not succumb to Iago if there were not an innate quality within him which is hospitable to the Iago "poison." There is a similarity here to Mac-beth and his hospitality to the temptation of the witches. Othello, however, asks "Who can control his fate?" (V,ii, 265). He may well be mistaken in his interpretation of his own tragedy, as he is about some other things. Nevertheless there is a crushing amount of coin-cidence and unlucky timing in the play; and fate (as in the loss of the handkerchief, a handkerchief rich in ominous history) cannot be entirely ruled out.

Nor can Iago be ruled out. Is he merely an externalization of some evil in Othello? Or the Vice (a mischievous tempter) of the moral-ity play? Or the devil who comes only (as in Marlowe's *Doctor Faustus*) to a person ready for him? He may be partly all these things, but he is also a superlatively interesting character in his own right, and the reader should never overlook, in his private scrutiny of the play, that it is the role of Iago that has come off best on the stage.

Even in the study, Iago's inscrutability is one of the great mysteries of dramatic literature. Regardless of the findings of scholars, stu-dents of the play will probably forever argue about Iago's motiva-tion. Other questions also arise. Why should so unnecessary an evil be so hideously successful? Why must it involve Desdemona? Is Iago insane? Has he genius? Is he, on the contrary, extremely lim-ited in intelligence? These are some of the questions that students will always try to answer—even without any assurance of success. Iago's strategy in the great temptation scene (III,iii) is in itself enough to reward endless inquiry into the nature of evil and the power of suggestion, and to make us ask, as did Dostoevsky (see the selec-tion by Harold C. Goddard, Part II, Chapter 6), whether we would ourselves be safe from an attack of Iago's sort.

Many recent critics see in the play religious meanings. One in-terpreter, J. A. Bryant, has read the entire play as a Biblical allegory, with Cassio as Adam, Desdemona as Christ, and Othello as God.

We must not, however, judge theological interpretation in general on the basis of so difficult a reading. Much sober criticism has been given to the question of whether Othello is saved or damned at the end of the play.

All questions of meaning aside, the play will always deeply move audiences by its ardent and powerful poetry. No one who has ever heard the play will forget the music of its great speeches: the "Farewell" (III,iii, 347–357), the "Pontic sea" (III,iii, 453–460), "It is the cause, it is the cause, my soul" (V,ii, 1–22), and "Then must you speak/Of one that lov'd not wisely, but too well" (V,ii, 343–344). All these utterances are by Othello himself. All have both sonority and sensitivity. They remind us of what we must never forget: that regardless of the cleverness and the virtuoso performance of Iago, it is Othello who is noble and beautiful. It is he who, through his poetic response to love and jealousy, compels us to see as a tragedy that which in a newspaper story might be sensational scandal.

2. Suggestions on Reading Shakespeare [1]

Shakespeare's plays are not difficult to read if it be remembered that they were written originally not to be read but to be played, that they contain a great deal of poetry, and, finally, that because they were composed more than three hundred years ago, they have some allusions with which we are not familiar and some words which we no longer use. Apart from these difficulties they may be read like modern plays for the story, the characters, and the philosophy of life which Shakespeare has packed into them. A careful reading for a complete understanding will demand, of course, frequent references to a glossary of Shakespearean words, but this necessity is no different from that of consulting a dictionary for unfamiliar words in a modern play. A careful reading, too, will demand close attention to the ideas expressed in the blank verse and other verse forms which Shakespeare used. Here practice will make the reading easy, and the poetic conventions employed by the playwright will soon become familiar. But even if an occasional word or allusion is lost, and an occasional bit of poetical dialogue remains obscure, the reader may get the cream of the play if only he adopt the right attitude of mind toward it. He must know something of what Shakespeare has tried to do in the play, and something also of his methods of work. He must know, too, what to look for so that his reading will not drift but will have a definite objective. In the following paragraphs are a few suggestions to guide him in his reading.

To Shakespeare, a play was not a few printed pages of dialogue for the isolated reader but a vivid mimetic presentation of human conflict by impersonators on the open platform of the Elizabethan theatre for an alert audience of imaginative Londoners. [Shakespeare] made no attempt, moreover, to insist upon a complete *physical* representation of every detail of his play; on the contrary, in the burlesque of the craftsmen in *A Midsummer Night's Dream* he pokes glorious fun at the amateur Thespians who do insist that moonshine, wall, and lion must be physically presented. The men and women who flocked to the Globe Theatre formed an *audience,* not a crowd of *spectators;* they came to hear as well as to see,

[1] Reprinted from Homer A. Watt, Karl J. Holzknecht, and Raymond Ross, *Outlines of Shakespeare's Plays* (New York: Barnes & Noble, Inc., 1957).

4

and Shakespeare used their ears to suggest to their imaginations much that could not be physically represented, as he does, for example in the *Prologue* to *Henry V:*

> "Piece out our imperfections with your thoughts;
> Into a thousand parts divide one man,
> And make imaginary puissance;
> Think, when we talk of horses, that you see them
> Printing their proud hoofs i' the receiving earth."

Shakespeare staged his plays, that is, not only on the platform of the theatre but also in the lively minds of the men and women in his audience; to them he gave the symbols of life and conflict, and they expanded these symbols into full being. "The best in this kind," said Duke Theseus of the players, "are but shadows; and the worst are no worse, if imagination amend them."

To *read* a play of Shakespeare's well, it is really necessary to go a step beyond the practice of the man in the Globe audience, and to create in our own minds the whole of the play. To read a play vividly we must re-create on the stage of our imaginations the whole setting and atmosphere, the action, and the characters. Dialogue between two characters must be more than words divided into statement and response; it must be the vivid interchange of ideas between two distinct individuals whom we see, as Hamlet carried the image of his father, in our "mind's eye." Moreover, we must be alert for every verbal suggestion that can help us to make our reconstruction of the play. So when the gentle King Duncan, coming to the castle of Macbeth, remarks,

> "This castle hath a pleasant seat; the air
> Nimbly and sweetly recommends itself
> Unto our gentle senses,"

lo, the castle must rise in our imaginations as vividly as ever it did on theatrical canvas. Similarly, when Macbeth demands angrily of the frightened servant who has come to report that the English soldiers are advancing against the stronghold,

> "The devil damn thee black, thou cream-faced loon!
> Where gott'st thou that goose look?"

we must realize with the eye and the ear of the mind the desperate, raging king and the trembling servant, "whey-faced" with terror. To read a play of Shakespeare's effectively, therefore, is actually to stage it on the platforms of our imaginations; only thus will the dramatic conflict be more than a faint and far-off thing and the characters more than bloodless and impersonal wraiths. When we pick up our Shakespeares we must not read "words, words, words"; we must re-create ideas, images, backgrounds, characters, conflicts, life.

Fortunately, Shakespeare did more than most modern dramatists to help his reader make this dramatic reconstruction. In fact, from one point of view his plays are very easy to read; he has taken his audience so completely into his confidence that they can follow his play-story as easily as though it were a fairy-tale. For the audience there are no mysteries or surprises in the play; the characters may be fooled and puzzled, but the members of the audience never are. For the reader the disguise is never complete; when Julia and Rosalind and Viola put on male garb, they may disappear from the knowledge of their lovers, but the reader knows that a girl's heart is beating beneath the doublet of the page or the smock of the shepherd. Similarly, *Hamlet* and *Macbeth* are not murder mysteries, nor is the villainy of Iago or of Iachimo kept dark from the audience. In the practical jokes of the comedies the reader always shares as a participant; Malvolio may be trapped, fat Falstaff may be derided by the merry wives, and Benedick and Beatrice may be tricked into matrimony, but the audience is invariably "in" on these jests and derives its delight from laughing at the blind folly of the poor dupes. Thus Shakespeare's plots are always open and easy to reconstruct on the stage of the imagination.

Even the simplest of Shakespeare's plays will repay a double reading. It is best to read the play rapidly once for the story and a second time for plot structure, characterization, and other elements which an honest reader will want to consider. The first reading should be done in the manner indicated, reproducing the play in the imagination. The play, in other words, should be read *as a drama,* not as a novel or an essay. The second reading may be done more slowly and more methodically with the attention alert for whatever technique of playwrighting and other elements are to be noted. This study-reading should be done, of course, with pencil in hand to make annotations on a convenient pad or even in the margin of the book and to underline passages that seem significant for any reason. For what in this closer reading should the student look? A few of the most essential elements follow.

The reader may determine first what manner or type of play he is reading, for in Shakespeare's day the distinctions were kept rather carefully in mind although Shakespeare tended more than did most of his contemporary playwrights to mix his forms. The basic division into comedy, tragedy, and history is made by the conventional grouping in the usual editions. But such division does not go far enough. *Henry V* and *Richard II,* for example, are both history plays, but the first is epic and the second tragic in character. Again, *As You Like It* and *Twelfth Night* are both romantic comedies, but the first is, in addition, a pastoral comedy, whereas the second is not. *The Taming of the Shrew* is a farce; *Love's Labor's Lost* is a court comedy of a social type. Shakespeare was essentially a romanticist; that is, most of his plays deal with events in a romantic and vague past and in a foreign country—often Greece, Rome, Italy, France. But the plays contain, nevertheless, much that is realistic. His dukes are not really Athenian, or Italian, or French, but English; his mobs are not Roman, or Italian, but London; and in many of his plays he ignores the early date of the action by bringing in contemporary episodes, backgrounds, and characters, as he does in the Boar's-Head Tavern scenes in *Henry IV.* All of these pastoral, romantic, and realistic elements the reader may wish to note before turning his attention particularly to plot, characters, and background.

Shakespeare's plots, as has been said above, are not particularly complicated or difficult to follow; on the contrary, they are usually simple and compact. A few of the history plays, like *King John* and *Henry V,* seem to have no particular climax that results from the issue of a conflict between individuals; and a few of his romances, like *Cymbeline* and *Pericles,* are straggling and loose in structure. But these are exceptions; the majority of the plays follow a rather definite pattern which is easily discernible. One might suppose that since Shakespeare seldom took the trouble to make his own basic plots but borrowed here and there from histories, prose romances, old plays, and even poems, his plots would invariably be what their originals are. This is not, however, true; he did not hesitate to change, add, and omit details and characters to suit his sense of craftsmanship with the result that he often made an excellent drama out of conventional and unpromising materials. It is good fun for the reader to compare a play of Shakespeare's with its source, but such comparison is not necessary for an understanding of the play, and at most it gives a sense of the facility with which the dramatist erected his striking structures on old foundations. Thus in *Henry IV* he makes Prince Hal and Hotspur—the grand rivals—of the same age, whereas Hotspur was actually some years older than the Prince's father; in *As You Like It*, again, he has the usurping duke reformed instead of killed in battle with his abused brother; in *Othello* Desdemona is strangled to death by her own husband instead of being struck down with a sand-filled stocking in the hands of the villainous ensign. Shakespeare is always quite original, therefore, in *dramatizing* his materials.

The simplicity of the plots consists ordinarily in their following a simple formula. Like all good drama, the plays have their bases in human conflict—in tragedy, a losing conflict, in comedy, a less serious one which has a happy conclusion. At the beginning of the play the audience is presented with an unstable condition which has existed for some time, and which continues to prevail in various aspects until it reaches its climax either in a tragic crash or in a happy and harmonious stability. In tragedy, the conflict has its poisonous roots in one or more of the grand passions which tear the hearts of kings, princes, and great generals—vaulting ambition, hate, greed, and other vultures of the soul which rest not until they have destroyed their victim. In comedy, the conflict is milder—a love tilt, perhaps; the turn of Fortune's wheel that restores a banished duke to his throne; the chance that puts twin brothers into the same city to be a source of confusion to their friends and relations. In comedy, the play usually begins with a number of separations, husband and wife, two brothers, brother and sister, two lovers, parents and child; it concludes with happy unions and reunions. It is not easy to reduce all of Shakespeare's plays to a single formula, but if we omit certain of the history plays, the rest may be said to present—often with considerable irony—to an audience wise as the gods, the spectacle of blind humanity forced to grope through a fog of uncertainty to a predestined doom in the tragedies or to light and happiness in the comedies. The tragedy ends with death; the comedy usually with marriage. The death-knell is as characteristic of one as the wedding-bell is of the other. The reader of the plays will readily note these essential features and patterns, for even play synopses will reveal them.

A play synopsis may not reveal, however, Shakespeare's frequent device of developing sub-plots, side-plots, and parallel plots in such a way as to strengthen the reader's understanding and emotional appreciation of the main plot. These secondary plots are never in Shakespeare's plays, as they are often in those of his contemporary playwrights, simply appendages to the main action; they are invariably and economically welded into it so that the total effect is that of one play and not that of two or more plays in one. The reader will want to note, of course, just what these various plots are, and by what methods they are woven into the texture of the whole. An illustration or two may make clearer this particular structural device. The story of *As You Like It* has to do with the disagreements of two sets of brothers,—in the main plot, older men, of whom one has exiled the duke, his brother, and, in the parallel plot, younger men, of whom the older has driven the younger into banishment. The two exiled brothers are ultimately followed into their place of banishment by the two villains, but both oppressors have a change of heart so that the banished men return home in happiness. The main plot is linked to the secondary plot not only by this obvious parallelism but further by the fact that the two brothers in the minor plot marry respectively the two daughters of the royal brothers of the major plot. In tragedy there are similar plot parallels. *King Lear,* for example, may be characterized as a tragedy of filial ingratitude. In the main plot, Lear disinherits his youngest daughter in favor of her two hypocritical sisters, who turn him out of doors as soon as they have come safely into full possession of his kingdom. In the minor plot, the Earl of Gloucester is tricked into disinheriting his loyal and legitimate son for a bastard son, who turns upon his father. The link in these two plots comes with the tiger queens' abuse of Gloucester and with their lust for the wicked bastard. In reading Shakespeare's plays the various plot-lines of the story and their relationship one to another must be carefully considered.

Shakespeare's plots, as has been frequently pointed out, have their roots in his characters. That is to say, in spite of the intervention of the Goddess of Chance, the events grow out of the moods and emotions of the main characters. Thus there is a dramatic harmony between persons and events so that things happen as they do because characters are what they are. It is amusing fun to shift characters from play to play, and to try to determine what would happen with the new actors in the plot. Just how, for example, would Rosalind act in Viola's place, and what would happen to the King of Denmark if Macbeth or Othello were in Hamlet's black doublet and hose? The outcome of these fancies is to realize that the action is exactly what might be expected with the characters in any given play what they are. A knowledge of the main characters is, therefore, highly important for an understanding of the action. How may the characters be analyzed?

Human beings reveal themselves in numerous ways. We know them by what they say, by their manner of saying it, and, often enough, by their silences or failure to say anything under given circumstances. We know them, too, by their actions, and even by their failure to act on occasions. We know them from what others say about them in statements which reveal both the speaker and the object of his comments. They are revealed to us, finally, by the device of contrasting them with others, by what is known technically as the use of character *foils*.

The first mentioned of these methods of revelation hardly needs elaboration. Shakespeare has often been called coarse because some of his characters are frank in their language. Actually he is only logical; he would have his hostlers, his prostitutes, his innkeepers, his rogues use the speech of their breeding and their trade and not that of ladies and gentlemen of the court. Similarly, his pedants talk like pedants, his soldiers like soldiers, his kings and queens like royalty. Beyond these group indications, however, the individual characteristics of his men and women are revealed by their speech. We could hardly understand the soul of Hamlet without his self-revealing soliloquies or his almost equally revealing conversations with his friend Horatio. Indeed, Shakespeare has a trick of providing many of his major characters—Portia, for instance—with confidants into whose ears they may pour their secrets. And as they speak so do they act or fail to act, the gentlemen like gentlemen, the rascals like rascals, kings royally if sometimes criminally, commoners according to their light and training. Again, characters are frequently characterized by those who speak about them. "These tedious old fools," says Hamlet of the boresome Polonius; and he stigmatizes Rosencrantz and Guildenstern as "adders fang'd." He is himself described in one of his distracted moods by Ophelia,

> "with his doublet all unbraced:
> No hat upon his head; his stockings fouled,
> Ungartered and down-gyved to his ankle;
> Pale as his shirt; his knees knocking each other;
> And with a look so piteous in purport
> As if it had been loosed out of hell
> To speak of horrors."

So Portia describes her lovers; Enobarbus, his emperor and "the serpent of the Nile"; and Macduff, the "hell-hound" usurper. All these characterizations the careful reader will wish to note, even though they may be as short as the epithet just quoted.

To one method of characterization Shakespeare seemed to have been especially partial; it is that of providing his major characters with contrasting opposites or *foils* designed to set them off. Sometimes the contrast is physical; Falstaff is fat, Shallow is thin; Hermia is short and dark, Helena is tall and fair. Usually, however, the contrast is one of temperament. Thus Claudio is reserved and cold, Benedick is alert and mercurial; Adriana is impatient and shrewish, her sister is calm and cool-headed. Occasionally the foils are of great importance and are carried throughout the entire play. Thus it is in *Hamlet*, where three men of different temperaments are all faced with the problem of avenging the death of a father. For fear that the audience may miss the comparison, indeed, Shakespeare has Prince Hamlet himself point out the resemblance of his own situation to that of Fortinbras and of Laertes. The question is this: How will each man solve the same problem? Hamlet himself, the man who thinks without acting, delays; Laertes, the man who acts without thinking, plunges; and the two tragic figures perish on the same poisoned sword, leaving the kingdom to Fortinbras, the cool-headed, balanced Norwegian who plans and acts in due proportion and at appropriate times for each. To drop Fortinbras from the play, as is done in most modern productions, is like knocking one leg from a tripod.

The background of the play, as has been said earlier [see p. 5], cannot be secured from any elaborate description of the setting such as those which embellish many modern printed plays. Locale and atmosphere come out of the mouths of the speakers and must be reconstructed from the dialogue. An assembling of these allusions and longer descriptions will reveal the essential appropriateness of the setting and the care with which the background has been made to harmonize with plot and characters. The blasted heath for the witches, the gloomy castle of Elsinore for the lone sentinel and the ghost in armor, the furious storm on the moor for the maddened King Lear and his ragged followers, the pleasant Forest of Arden for the exiles, Olivia's garden for Toby and Aguecheek—these and others too numerous to mention should be studied for their contribution to the whole and for their share in the structural unity which is one of Shakespeare's essential characteristics.

PART TWO: ANALYSIS OF THE PLAY

1. Scene-by-Scene Synopsis of *Othello*

While studying or reviewing a play, the reader often wishes to recall the main events and sequence of the action or to locate characters quickly. The following chapter provides a ready and convenient reference for this purpose.

CHARACTERS

Duke of Venice.
BRABANTIO, [a Senator,] father to *Desdemona*.
Senators.
GRATIANO, [brother to *Brabantio*,] } two noble Venetians.
LODOVICO, [kinsman to *Brabantio*,] }
OTHELLO, the Moor, [in the service of Venice].
CASSIO, [his] honorable Lieutenant.
IAGO, [his Ancient,] a villain.
RODERIGO, a gull'd [Venetian] gentleman.
MONTANO, [former] Governor of Cyprus.
CLOWN, [servant to *Othello*].
DESDEMONA, [daughter to Brabantio and] wife to *Othello*.
EMILIA, wife to *Iago*.
BIANCA, a courtesan, [in love with *Cassio*].
Sailor, [Messenger, Herald, Officers, Gentlemen, Musicians, Attendants].

Scene.—VENICE; CYPRUS.

I,i. Late at night, on a street in Venice, Iago and Roderigo are discussing Othello's recent elopement with Desdemona. Roderigo, who has been one of Desdemona's suitors, protests indignantly against Iago's concealing the affair from him, intimating that Iago's loyalty now lies with Othello. In defense, Iago declares that since he was passed over in the choice of Cassio as Othello's new lieutenant, he has every reason to hate the Moor. He exalts his own duplicity: in the public

12

eye seeming a dutiful servant, but privately seeking his own "peculiar end." Meanwhile, they have reached Brabantio's house and wake him to tell that his daughter has eloped with Othello. Iago slips away as Brabantio sets off with Roderigo to find his missing daughter and Othello.

I,ii. Shortly afterward, on another street, Iago has joined Othello when Cassio delivers a message from the Duke of Venice that summons Othello immediately to a military council. Then, as Brabantio and Roderigo enter, accompanied by armed officers, the scene nearly erupts into violence. Brabantio accuses Othello of having bewitched Desdemona and demands that he be thrown at once into prison. With dignity Othello manages to pacify the others and persuades Brabantio to take his complaint before the Duke.

I,iii. Later in the night the Duke and his Senators, in council, are discussing discrepancies in the several reports of a threatening Turkish fleet. Othello, Brabantio, Iago, Roderigo, and others enter. Brabantio again alleges that nothing but witchcraft could have induced his daughter to marry Othello, but this Othello denies. The Duke sends attendants to fetch Desdemona, and Iago accompanies them at Othello's request. Desdemona is called to speak for herself; in the meanwhile Othello tells how he met and courted his new wife and how he fascinated her with the accounts of his own travels and adventures. Desdemona arrives and gently resolves the dispute by acknowledging split loyalties to her father and to her new husband, but making it clear that she now belongs to Othello. Brabantio bitterly rejects his daughter and also the Duke's attempts to console him. The Duke returns his attention to the Turks and directs Othello to defend Cyprus and become its new governor. Desdemona will follow later under Iago's protection to join Othello in Cyprus. As all the others leave, Iago and Roderigo are once again alone. Despite Roderigo's threats of suicide, Iago revitalizes his hope and fools him into thinking that he may still win Desdemona. Left alone, Iago admits to himself that money and amusement are his real reasons for befriending Roderigo. Then he begins to plan the deception of Othello which will afford him revenge for his many grievances against the Moor.

II,i. A storm at sea has crippled the Turkish fleet and delayed the course of Othello's voyage. At Cyprus, Montano greets Cassio, whose ship is the first to arrive; shortly afterward, Iago's ship also arrives with Desdemona on board. To assuage Desdemona's anxiety for Othello's safety, Iago jokes and composes verses, and Cassio also distracts her attention in an amiable conversation. Iago privately notes

Cassio's behavior toward Desdemona and plans to entrap him. Finally, Othello arrives, joyously reunites with Desdemona, and embraces her. When the others have left, Iago convinces the foolish Roderigo that Desdemona actually loves Cassio and urges him to pick a fight with the lieutenant that same night. Once more alone, Iago discloses his vague suspicions about Othello's and Cassio's affairs with his own wife, Emilia.

II,ii. Othello's Herald proclaims a night of feasting and festivity to celebrate the destruction of the Turkish fleet and the wedding of Othello to Desdemona.

II,iii. Othello retires for the night with Desdemona, leaving Cassio in charge of the nightwatch. In a hall of the castle in Cyprus, against the background of the night's merrymaking, Iago succeeds with wine and song in making Cassio drunk and quarrelsome. Urged by Iago to start an altercation, Roderigo follows Cassio offstage; quickly the two reappear fighting. Montano interferes in an attempt to stop them and accuses Cassio of being drunk. Enraged, Cassio turns on him and wounds him as Roderigo hurries to sound the alarm. Disturbed by the bell, Othello returns, halts the fighting, and demands to know what caused it. Upon Iago's seemingly reluctant description of the disturbance, Othello finds Cassio at fault and immediately discharges him. Iago and Cassio remain as Montano is led off and the others follow. Cassio, sobered, regrets the loss of his office and reputation, but Iago persuades him to regain Othello's favor indirectly with Desdemona's help. After Cassio leaves, Iago gloats over his successful, although seemingly innocent, scheming. Roderigo returns, sore and full of complaints after his beating. Iago soothes his impatience with platitudes and points out their success in causing Cassio's discharge. They part as day breaks.

III,i. Cassio installs some musicians to serenade the newly wedded couple. Othello's Clown enters and with much humor asks them to stop playing. Iago arrives and helps Cassio arrange a private meeting with Desdemona. After Iago leaves, his wife Emilia enters and, at Cassio's request, takes him to talk with Desdemona.

III, ii. Othello tells Iago that he will inspect the fortification of the Castle with some gentlemen and requests that Iago meet him there.

III, iii. In the Castle garden, Desdemona promises Cassio that she will do all in her power on his behalf. As Othello and Iago enter, Cassio, feeling ill-at-ease, leaves hurriedly. As Othello is approaching his wife, he notices Cassio's departure; Iago quickly takes the opportunity to draw Othello's attention to Cassio's "guilty-like" leave-taking. Desdemona launches at once into her petition for Cassio, continuing good-humoredly, yet insistently, until Othello grants her plea. Iago's insinuations begin as Desdemona and Emilia withdraw. When, in reply to Iago's calculated questions, Othello says that Cassio was often instrumental in Othello's courtship of Desdemona, Iago acts astonished. Othello asks him to make plain what he has been thinking, but Iago adroitly evades the direct question until he has fully aroused Othello's curiosity. Then he cunningly warns Othello against jealousy, the "green-ey'd monster." But Othello answers confidently that he will harbor no suspicions unless they can be proved. Ostensibly reassured, Iago openly suggests an affair between Cassio and Desdemona; in countless ways he begins to undermine Othello's faith in Desdemona's innocence. After Iago has left, Othello is temporarily reassured when Desdemona returns. She tries to soothe his aching head with her handkerchief, but he throws it down; and as they depart, it is left behind. Emilia picks up the strawberry-embroidered handkerchief, Othello's first gift to Desdemona, and gives it to Iago. Othello re-enters, his mind at ferment on the seeds of doubt planted by Iago. He demands proof, immediate and positive. Iago claims that while spending a night with Cassio he overheard Cassio talking in a dream of making love to Desdemona. He also says that he has seen Cassio wipe his beard with a handkerchief embroidered with strawberries. Enraged by this fabricated evidence, Othello sinks to his knees. He is joined by Iago, and together they vow sacred revenge. On rising, Othello promotes Iago to be his lieutenant.

III,iv. Standing in front of the castle, Desdemona sends the Clown to bring Cassio to her. When Othello enters, she again takes up Cassio's cause, but Othello's only concern is the handkerchief. Desdemona lies, saying that she has not lost it, for Othello has told her that the handkerchief possesses magical power and that its loss would be a misfortune. Othello leaves angrily when she cannot produce it. Iago and Cassio enter; together with Desdemona and Emilia, they seem to be at a loss to explain Othello's distemper. When the others have left, Cassio meets Bianca and gives her the handkerchief that he found in his room, asking her to make a copy of the embroidery. Bianca is disturbed at his neglecting her, but she nevertheless agrees to do it. Cassio tells her to leave.

IV,i. Othello rages and falls into a trance when Iago tells him that Cassio has admittedly lain with Desdemona. Just then Cassio enters, but Iago asks him to withdraw and to return in a short time, since Othello has suffered an epileptic fit. Othello recovers and agrees to hide so that he can watch Cassio as Iago draws him out in conversation about Desdemona. After Cassio's return, Iago engages him in a joking conversation about Bianca's infatuation for him. Othello, who can hear nothing, misinterprets his smiles and gestures, believing they refer to Desdemona. Bianca enters and angrily returns the handkerchief to Cassio, saying that she refuses to copy another woman's present. She leaves and Cassio follows in order to appease her. Again Othello is enraged at this seemingly direct proof of Desdemona's infidelity. At Iago's suggestion, he agrees to strangle Desdemona in her bed while Iago promises to murder Cassio. Lodovico has arrived on a ship from Venice bringing a letter from the Duke. He enters with Desdemona. As Othello reads the letter which orders his return to Venice and appoints Cassio Governor of Cyprus, Desdemona tells Lodovico of the breach between Othello and Cassio. Desdemona's sympathy for Cassio again angers Othello; he strikes and torments her and she leaves weeping. Othello, who has now lost all self-control, also leaves.

IV,ii. Questioned by Othello, Emilia swears that Desdemona is chaste. He sends for Desdemona and asks her directly to swear that she has been faithful. She professes her innocence, but Othello will not believe her. He accuses her of being a whore and a strumpet. When her husband leaves, Desdemona, stunned, sends for Iago and asks him how she can clear herself. Iago tells her to be calm and patient since some official matter must temporarily have disturbed Othello. Desdemona and Emilia leave as Roderigo enters. Iago convinces him that Cassio must be killed and together they plot the murder.

IV,iii. Othello orders Desdemona to go to bed unattended. As Emilia prepares her for bed, her mind is preoccupied with sad thoughts. She sings a song, "Willow," that she has learned from her mother's maid, who loved a man who went mad. In contrast with Emilia's worldly opinions, Desdemona swears that she would never abuse her husband.

V,i. Late that same night on a street in Cyprus, Iago and Roderigo are waiting for their opportunity to murder Cassio. As Cassio enters, Roderigo's first pass at him fails, and instead Cassio wounds Roderigo. Iago rushes out and wounds Cassio in the leg without being seen. Othello, passing by, hears Cassio call out and so believes that Iago's half of the plot has succeeded. Lodovico and Gratiano enter and, after them, Iago with a light. Both wounded men are still alive; Iago comforts Cassio and stabs Roderigo mortally in the dark. Bianca enters, and Iago tries to implicate her since Cassio ate supper at her house nearby. Cassio and Roderigo are carried off. Emilia enters, and Iago dispatches her to Othello to tell him what has occurred.

V,ii. Desdemona is nearly asleep in her bedchamber as Othello enters. He extinguishes his candle and, filled with regrets, he gives her one last kiss. Desdemona is awakened and, realizing his intent, she pleads for mercy. But he will not be stopped and smothers her. Emilia pounds at the door bringing news of Cassio's wounding, but Othello does not let her in to deliver Iago's message until Desdemona has apparently died. With her last breath, Desdemona tries to hide Othello's guilt. Othello confesses the murder to Emilia, telling her that her own husband convinced him that Desdemona was a strumpet. Horrified, Emilia tells him that Iago has told him lies only, and then she rushes out to publicize the crime. Montano, Gratiano, Iago, and others enter. Othello begins to tell of his suspicions based upon the handkerchief, but Emilia, realizing his mistake, explains that she stole it herself for Iago. Infuriated, Iago kills his own wife as Othello is disarmed by Montano. Othello finds another sword and wounds Iago for his deception. Little by little the full circumstances are exposed. In complete despair over Desdemona's death, Othello stabs himself with a concealed dagger, as the others look on in consternation, and dies kissing Desdemona.

2. Sources

Elizabethan England was ready for Shakespeare's tragedy of jealousy and divided love. Before the production of *Othello* (1604), the news had already created its own Moor of Venice and the "gentle Desdemona" as well:

(1.) Christopher Moro, a heroic Venetian general in mourning for his recently deceased wife, returned to Venice in 1508 from the lord-lieutenancy of Cyprus, after the failure of a Turkish attack on the island.

(2.) San Pietro di Bastelica, an Italian adventurer of great distinction in the service of France, in 1563 returned abruptly from a mission to Constantinople (to beg assistance for the Corsicans from the Turks) because of artfully circulated reports of his wife's infidelity. Thereupon, after a scene of mingled tenderness and ferocity on his part and gentle submission on hers, he asked pardon for the deed he was about to commit and strangled her with her handkerchief.

It is quite possible that these events, which resemble certain elements within *Othello,* may have fired Shakespeare's imagination, thus influencing his conception of the tragedy. This, of course, we can never know. His literary source for the plot is, however, certain.[1]

In 1565, a novelist, poet, and university professor named Giraldi Cinthio compiled and published in Montregale, Sicily, a "philosophical" work entitled *Hecatommithi* (The Hundred Fables). In it, ten moral virtues or their opposites are illustrated by ten appropriate tales from contemporary life. *Othello,* in skeleton form and with minor variations, appears in the seventh novel of the third decade which deals (appropriately) with the "Unfaithfulness of Husbands and Wives."

No one has established whether Shakespeare read the original Italian version (there were none in English at the time). A few Italian phrases are followed more closely than their equivalents in the available French translation. At any rate, it is interesting to note how he combined elements of Cinthio's prose tale with his own poetic imagination and dramatic art. The following summary will trace plot development in this moral fable in relation to corresponding references from *Othello.*[2]

Cinthio gives a name to none of his prototypes of Shakespeare's characters except the heroine, who is called Disdemona. Othello is simply "the Moor" ("Moro"), Iago "the Ensign" ("alfiero"), Cassio "the head of a band" ("Capo di squadra"), Emilia "the Ensign's wife," and Bianca "a courtesan." Roderigo is barely suggested by the soldier whom we are told the Capo struck (II,iii, 153); the clown, Gratiano, and other Venetian nobles are omitted entirely. Shakespeare's Duke may have been drawn from Cinthio's Signory of Venice, who thought much of the Moor's bravery and military genius (I,iii, 222–225). And it is evident that Cinthio's reference to the "parental opposition" arising from Disdemona's marriage provided the inspiration for Shakespeare's memorable Brabantio and the trial in Act I, Scene iii.

---

[1] Other literary sources, including Ariosto's *Orlando Furioso,* Philemon Holland's translation of Pliny's *Natural History,* and Sir Lewes Lewkenor's translation of Cardinal Contareno's *The Commonwealth and Government of Venice,* are suggested by Kenneth Muir, *Shakespeare's Sources,* I (London: Methuen & Co., 1957), pp. 122–140.

[2] A generally satisfactory translation of Cinthio—the one most frequently consulted for the present summary—is that of John Edward Taylor (1855).

As the story opens, we learn that the Moor is highly regarded by the Signory of Venice for his bravery and military genius, both of which have advanced the interests of the State. (See above.) Cinthio also describes a virtuous lady of great beauty, Disdemona, who falls in love with the Moor because of his "virtù" (valor) and, despite parental opposition (I,iii), marries him. They live in Venice in complete love and harmony for an indefinite time, but certainly longer than the brief period of the marriage in Shakespeare.

One day the Signory made a change in the troops used to maintain Cyprus (Cinthio, unlike Shakespeare, suggests no reason for the change), and appointed the Moor as commander (I,iii, 48–49). The Moor's delight at this appointment was marred only by the prospect of leaving Disdemona in Venice, or jeopardizing her safety on a tumultuous sea voyage. But Disdemona minimized the dangers and persuaded her husband to take her with him (I,iii, 260). The Moor, thus encouraged, embraced his wife with the tragically ironic words, "God keep you long in the love, dear wife," and then embarked with her and all his troops to Cyprus.

Cinthio now introduces three more of his characters, among whom is the Ensign, described as "a man of handsome figure, but of the most depraved nature in the world." The Ensign had likewise taken his own wife to Cyprus (II,i, 97) and she was much loved by Disdemona, who spent a great part of the day with her.

We are told that the Ensign, as part of the soldiery, was highly esteemed by the Moor, who had no inkling of his malevolent nature (I,iii, 405–406). Also in the same company was the Capo, likewise esteemed by the Moor, who often came to his house and dined with him and his wife. Since Disdemona knew that her husband loved him, she showed him much kindness and consideration, which greatly pleased the Moor. But the "wicked" Ensign, despite the fidelity he owed his wife and the loyalty he owed the Moor, fell passionately in love with Disdemona and "bent all his thoughts to achieve his conquest."

Devoted as she was to the Moor, Disdemona showed no interest in the Ensign's overtures, thus turning his love into bitter hate. He concluded that Disdemona must love the Capo and began to plot against both their lives.

After considering various schemes, all "wicked," he decided to accuse Disdemona of infidelity and to represent the Capo as her paramour (I,iii, 398–402). But knowing the Moor's extraordinary love for Disdemona and his deep friendship for the Capo, the Ensign craftily began to wait for an opportunity to enact his foul scheme.

Such an opportunity arose for the villainous Ensign when the Capo drew a sword upon a soldier of the guard, struck him, and thus was deprived of his rank by the Moor (II,iii, 248–249).

Disdemona took the affair much to heart and, grieving for the loss of friendship between the Moor and the Capo, begged her husband to restore the Capo to his former rank (III,iii, 46–47). The Moor unwittingly played into the Ensign's hands by telling him of Disdemona's intercession. Armed with this information, the Ensign was now able to weave his treachery and said, "Perhaps the Lady may have good reason to look kindly on him (the Capo)." Immediately suspicious, the Moor asked why this was so, but the Ensign refused to give details (III,iii, 106–116), saying that he would not step between husband and wife. His only admonition was for the Moor to observe his wife and the Capo (III,iii, 196–200), and to see for himself.

The Ensign's words cast the Moor into a deep melancholy, which was further piqued by Disdemona's entreaties for a reconciliation between him and the Capo (for example, III,iv, 86–88). Recognizing that his wife had repeated her petition in the Capo's favor, he thought that Disdemona was unfaithful and went to the Ensign, very sad and tormented (III,iii, 335), and tried to get him to speak more openly. The Ensign, claiming he did not wish to displease the Moor, then gave way and said: ". . . you must know then that it is a serious matter for your Lady to see the Capo in disfavor with you, because of the pleasure which she gets with him when he comes to your home, for your blackness already displeases her." (Perhaps III,iii, 228–238.)

These words cruelly pierced the Moor's wounded soul, and with a fierce look he demanded that the Ensign produce proof of his lady's infidelity (III,iii, 359–363, 386–390, 409). But the clever Ensign claimed that the Capo had often tasted Disdemona's body when he was in the Moor's favor, but now that he was out of it, he vented his appetites with greater caution. "But yet I do not lose hope of being able to make you see what you are loth to believe."

The unhappy Moor went home, while the Ensign began to plot a means by which he could make his tale more credible. Finally, the rogue hit upon a new device. Since Disdemona often came to visit his wife, he had noticed her wearing an elaborate handkerchief, embroidered in a Moorish design. He knew that the Moor had given it to Disdemona, and that the handkerchief was precious to both of

them. His next step was to steal it (III,iii, 305–319), thus laying a
snare for Disdemona's ruin.

The Ensign had a little girl three years of age whom Disdemona
much loved, and one day when the Moor's wife was visiting this villain's house, he took the little girl in his arms and put her on the
lady's lap. She pressed the child to her bosom, while the Ensign removed the handkerchief from her girdle so cunningly that she did not
notice it at all. In a few days Disdemona discovered the loss, and finding the handkerchief nowhere, became fearful that the Moor might
ask her about it, as he often did.

With perfect timing, the Ensign went to the Capo's quarters and
left the handkerchief at the head of his bed (III,iii, 321–322). The
Capo discovered it the following morning and, knowing it belonged
to the Moor's wife, considered how to return it to her. Fortune was
in league with the Ensign, for as the Capo knocked on her door, the
Moor returned home and, hearing a noise, went to the window. In a
furious voice he asked who was knocking. The Capo, afraid that the
Moor would do him harm, ran away without answering. The Moor
rushed into the street and searched everywhere until finally, enraged,
he returned to the house and asked Disdemona who the visitor was.
The lady answered that she did not know, which was true. The Moor
restrained his growing fury and went to the Ensign, begging him to
find out all he could from the Capo. The Ensign promised to do so,
happy at this new turn of events.

Consequently, he arranged a conference between himself and the
Capo with the Moor looking on unnoticed (IV,i, 75–84). The Ensign,
speaking with the Capo of anything but Disdemona, made a great
show of astonishment, gesticulating wildly, as though hearing unusual
things. After the Capo left, the Moor asked the Ensign what had been
said to him. "He has hidden nothing from me," the Ensign said. "He
told me that he has enjoyed your wife every time that, by your absence, you have given him the opportunity, and that the last time he
was with her she gave him that handkerchief which you gave her
when you married her." (III,iii, 437–439.)

The Moor thanked the Ensign and supposed that the proof of
Disdemona's infidelity rested on the handkerchief. Accordingly he
asked his lady for it at dinner, and his suspicions were confirmed
when Disdemona, growing red with embarrassment, could not produce
it (III,iv, 85–97). Thereafter the Moor began to meditate on how
to put his wife and the Capo to death. He asked the Ensign to ar-

range that he might see the Capo in possession of the handkerchief. The villain promised to show the truth of what he said.

Now the Capo had a wife who did wonderful embroidery on linen cambric and who, seeing the handkerchief and learning that it belonged to the Moor's wife and was to be returned to her, set about making one like it before the original was restored. While she was making it, the Ensign noticed that she stood in a window and could be seen by all from the street. He then drew the Moor's attention to this, and the Moor at last was fully convinced of his wife's guilt. He therefore planned with the Ensign to kill Disdemona and the Capo, and together they considered various forms of revenge, but could not settle on any one. The Ensign reluctantly agreed to kill the Capo (IV,i, 224–225), after accepting a large sum of money from the Moor.

And so one night, when the Capo was on the way to his courtesan, the Ensign attacked him, cut off his leg, and was about to finish the deed. But the Capo, accustomed to blood and death, drew his sword to defend himself, crying in a loud voice, "I am assassinated!" (V,i, 27.)

Hearing the approach of citizens and soldiers, the Ensign fled, and then turning around, pretended that he too was running toward the alarm. He saw the Capo's half-severed leg, and judging that he soon would die, feigned sympathy as though they were brothers (V,i, 56; 73).

Disdemona heard of the Capo's misfortune and expressed great sympathy, which further convinced the Moor of his wife's treachery. Later he and the Ensign discussed whether the lady should die by poison or the knife, until they hit on a plan which involved neither method.

From this point on, Cinthio's tale shows little resemblance to Shakespeare's tragedy. The Ensign devised a plan to secure Disdemona's death without suspicion falling on either himself or the Moor. He suggested beating her to death with a sand-filled stocking so that her body would show no signs of violence and then pulling down an already rotten timber of ceiling upon her, so that she would seem to have been killed by a falling rafter. The Moor and the Ensign carried out this plan successfully; but we are told that heaven will not allow the murderers of the gentle Disdemona to go unpunished.

One day the Moor, who loved Disdemona "more than his eyes," ran mad with grief and remorse and searched for her everywhere in the house. He longed to kill the Ensign, but dared not, fearing the "inviolable justice of the Signory of Venice," and instead cashiered him. Incited by the Ensign, the Capo later accused the Moor of murder, and the Moor was tortured by Venetian authorities, but would not confess (V,ii, 303–304). Condemned to lifelong exile, he was finally killed by Disdemona's relatives. The Ensign was not suspected. Later, in connection with another intrigue, he died under torture. After his death, his wife revealed the whole truth about the murder.

Cinthio's tale contains neither the heights of tragedy nor the flashing insights into character that we find in Shakespeare's *Othello*. This is no slur against the Italian writer, for the *Hecatommithi* are moral fables, not dramatic art, and it is significant that Disdemona points to the moral of *her* story when she declares to the Ensign's wife (Emilia) that her fate is a warning to Italian girls not to marry a man divided from them by race (la Natura), religion (il Cielo), and manner of life (il modo della vita).

Perhaps the most striking example of the differences between these two works is the way in which Cinthio's Moor is depicted in the final paragraphs. Unlike Othello, he does not regard Disdemona's death as his priestlike duty "else she'll betray more men," but merely as a suitable revenge for his injured pride. There is surely no real nobility in Cinthio's Moor—most particularly in the final paragraphs—whereas Shakespeare's Othello attains the dimensions of a tragic hero whose suffering consists in spiritual alienation from his wife. Cinthio hints at this alienation, but his Moor needs little motivation for the murder since the husbands of his world are fundamentally distrustful of their wives: "They are not ever jealous for the cause,/But jealous for they are jealous" (III,iv, 160–161).

Iago is likewise different from Cinthio's stock villain of the Italian school. The Ensign is motivated only by thwarted lust, whereas Iago's revenge supposedly stems from Cassio's promotion, lust for Desdemona (II,i, 300–302), and fear that the Moor has beguiled his own wife— ". . . the thought whereof/Doth, like a poisonous mineral, gnaw my inwards" (II,i, 305–306). It is interesting to note that both Iago's and the Ensign's plots contain all the elements of their own fantasies and fears. But what is more significant is the way in which Shakespeare has converted the details of a flat prose tale, with little character delineation, into the living tissue of tragic art.

3. Theme, Setting, Action

Theme. The theme of *Othello,* the play's principal claim upon our emotions, is jealousy. The word *jealous* (or *jealousy*) occurs fifteen times, an indication that the subject is talked about, the fatal emotion specified. But more important than the word is the idea as shown in character and action. Almost all the main characters are in some way jealous or are involved in the jealousy of others.

The emotion is of course most powerfully depicted as it affects the central character, Othello himself. In the Moor may be studied the four usual ingredients of this complex emotion: pride, love, hate, and uncertainty.

Othello is a proud man, though perhaps pride is not his dominant flaw, as G. R. Elliott has contended it is.[1] He is confident of his "perfect soul" (I,ii, 31) and is proud but not boastful about his noble birth (I,ii, 19–22). When he comes to suspect his wife (III,iii), he is especially troubled by the indignity of sharing her with others:

> I had rather be a toad
> And live upon the vapour of a dungeon
> Than keep a corner in the thing I love
> For others' uses. (III,iii, 270–273)

His last speech shows a vestige of noble pride. He has "done the state some service"; he is one who "lov'd not wisely, but too well." It is important to understand Othello's lofty self-esteem, because it is closely connected with his jealousy.

During the raging of the jealousy, love wars against hate. This is brought out in some of the most poignant speeches of III,iii, and the warfare leads to the final ingredient of jealousy: uncertainty. Othello at first thinks that the solution to jealousy will be an easy one: he need only convert love to hate. But he finds that the two emotions are inextricably blended, that he cannot give up loving the woman he now hates; and it is appropriate that the murder itself should be almost erotic. No longer able to stand the warfare of emotions, Othello stones his heart. In this seemingly emotionless state, he convinces himself that by killing Desdemona he will be a minister

---

[1] *Flaming Minister* (Durham, N. C.: Duke University Press, 1953).

of justice (cf. V,ii, 1–17). However, after Emilia has convinced him of his horrible error, emotion breaks through into consciousness again and Othello turns his hate momentarily upon himself before rising to the proud calm of his last speech. He finally reaches relief from what is for him the intolerable state of uncertainty.

Though jealousy is shown most heart-rendingly in Othello, and though the play would not be the tragedy it is if a different kind of hero had been afflicted, we must not assume that the study of jealousy in this play is limited to the hero. The motivating spirit of jealousy is Iago, and it is no accident that it is he who is most natively jealous. Othello, if we can believe his own testimony (V,ii, 345), is not easily jealous; but Iago is almost the embodiment of jealousy from the very start of the play. In him, however, we see only two of the customary four ingredients of jealousy: those of pride and hate. He can love, in a sense, but only himself. He has little uncertainty, because there is no war between love and hate.

If we consider Iago to be a genuine human being and not a morality play Vice or an incarnation of "motiveless malignity" (Coleridge), his jealousy, as well as his motivation, is difficult to account for. He may, as Marvin Rosenberg has interestingly suggested,[1] be a proud man chafing under the necessity for appearing pleasantly respectful to his superiors. This helps to account for his professional jealousy, his vexation at being disappointed in army promotion. But there are other factors that are irrational or abnormal. He *hates* almost without cause. Also, he feels the keenest of sexual jealousy although he is incapable of love. He is jealous about too many things to be a realistically wronged person, unless we consider, as perhaps we must, that he is insanely jealous. As a paranoid type, he would have delusions of both persecution and grandeur. There is, moreover, no question as to the genuineness of the anguish which Iago feels; it gnaws his "inwards" (II,i, 306). Also associated with his jealousy is a kind of morbid prurience. He suspects the worst of all women and delights in imagining lust in the virtuous Desdemona.

Is Iago, then, solely responsible for Othello's jealousy? If he were, Othello would not, as we have seen (Part I, Chapter 1), have what a Shakespearean hero normally has: freedom of choice. And we have also seen that Othello possesses, latently, the four ingredients of jealousy.

Other persons in the play who feel considerable jealousy are

[1] *The Masks of Othello* (Berkeley and Los Angeles: University of California Press, 1961), pp. 174–178.

Roderigo, Bianca, and possibly Brabantio. The most jealous of these is Roderigo, for his thwarted love for Desdemona leads him, with Iago's encouragement, to attempt murder.

Setting. Setting is not so important in *Othello* as it is in *King Lear* and *Macbeth.* The physical surroundings are not often described. What is more, there is no enlargement of the scene from the local and realistic to the supernatural. Atmosphere is, as we shall see in the next chapter, quite important, but it arises out of imagery rather than setting.

Nevertheless the two places in which *Othello* is set are distinguishable. The play commences in Venice and then, at the beginning of Act II, moves to Cyprus for the rest of the action.

Venice is the ultimate base of the action. All of the major characters except Othello and Cassio are Venetians, and they bring with them to Cyprus what they had become in Venice. Venice represents two things above all: a peaceful, law-abiding city and, according to some evidence, a city of sophisticated customs. The scene with the Duke and senators (I,iii) demonstrates the first of these. Venice, despite Brabantio's hysteria over his daughter's elopement, executes wise, impartial judgment, and all of its citizens except Iago are fair minded, even to the exotic and not always intelligible Othello. Concerning the sophistication of the Venetians, we hear about this only from Iago and perhaps from Brabantio's reference to the kind of suitors Desdemona had spurned: "The wealthy curled darlings of our nation" (I,ii, 68). Iago calls Desdemona "a supersubtle Venetian" (I,iii, 364); he also tells Othello:

> In Venice they do let heaven see the pranks
> They dare not show their husbands . . . (III,iii, 202–203)

Nothing in the play bears this out, but many in Shakespeare's England had learned from books and returning travelers to distrust Italians for their elegance and cunning. Certainly, we are meant to ascribe it to Desdemona's credit that she had rejected courtly and suave Venetian suitors in favor of the Moor, but we are not meant to condemn Venice as significantly overcivilized.

From the peaceful, protected, and refined society of Venice, the scene turns to Cyprus, "a town of war,/Yet wild, the people's hearts brimful of fear" (II,iii, 213–214). In courageously following her new and strange husband to Cyprus, Desdemona severs herself from her family and culture. When the crisis with her maddened husband occurs, she has no relatives to whom to turn. Cyprus for her brings ominous isolation. Like other islands in Shakespeare, it is also the scene of strange happenings. But they are not supernatural or an integral part of the atmosphere of the place. Without Iago, Cyprus would be a pleasant island.

Action. Othello is one of the most compactly structured of Shakespeare's tragedies. It has no subplot; very few of its episodes could be cut in a performance without doing violence to the play. Unlike *King Lear* or *Hamlet*, it achieves its power not by expansion but by compression. Everything focuses upon the single source of emotion and the intrigue which causes it. It is a domestic rather than a cosmic tragedy.

A part of the unity of design may be due to the fact that much of the drama is really a play-within-a-play, plotted and staged by Iago. Shakespeare elsewhere (as in *As You Like It, Hamlet,* and *The Tempest*) uses a character as dramatist, but never such a crazed character as Iago. Hazlitt called Iago "an amateur of tragedy in real life." Iago's plans for "revenge" take almost the form of an amateur theatrical, the sort of performance which the maddened Hieronimo devises, and acts in, in Thomas Kyd's enormously influential *The Spanish Tragedy*. But Hieronimo has a script. He knows the conclusion of his little play. Iago's production has an excitingly extemporaneous quality:

> 'Tis here, but yet confus'd.
> Knavery's plain face is never seen till us'd.
>   (II,i, 320–321)

Hence Iago, as well as the audience, does not know until the very end just what the conclusion to his drama will be. Along the way, he drafts for parts in his tragedy all sorts of persons (including even an anonymous "three lads of Cyprus"—II,iii, 57–61), appraising them with an insane, but cunning, dramatist's eye. He takes advantage, as a good dramatist should, of fortunate coincidences (like the hurried departure of Cassio at the beginning of III,iii). Probably, because of his mounting cast of characters and his increasing involvement in his own play, he does not at first foresee the extent of the catastrophe. It is unlikely, for example, that he plots the death of Desdemona. Moreover, actors get out of hand. Emilia, the wife whom he despises, steps out of her assigned minor role and proves to be the agent of his undoing.

Besides the device of the "play-within-a-play," Shakespeare shows his structural skill in the handling of time. The story of *Othello* required, troublesomely, both a rapid and a slow tempo. The story had to be so swift moving that Othello could not have leisure to study what was happening to him; it had to be sufficiently slow moving so that the events justifying his suspicions could plausibly have taken place. Shakespeare solved this problem—not perhaps with much conscious anxiety about it—by using two kinds of time: fast and slow.

The attentive reader begins to notice the two "clocks" only after the arrival in Cyprus. All the action from the beginning of Act II to the end of the play takes, according to several references to time, only thirty-three hours. This is the "fast time." But thirty-three hours—as Shakespeare must have realized—was not sufficient to justify Iago's accusation of repeated adultery. And one should notice that it is *adultery*, not premarital license, of which Desdemona is accused. There would have been no time for the alleged affair between Cassio and Desdemona either in Cyprus or in the brief period of elopement in Venice. Plausibility is achieved by "slow time." Slow time indicates a period in Cyprus of more than a week: Bianca upbraids Cassio for having been away from her so long; Lodovico has time to sail from Venice and reach Cyprus after the news of the Turkish rout has reached Venice.

Again, it should be stressed that this juggling of time was probably not fully deliberate on Shakespeare's part, any more than was his confusing arithmetic about Hamlet's age. He knew that in the theater the discrepancy goes unnoticed. But his dramatic sense impelled him simply to supply *hints* that both standards of time were possible. As a result we have both a fast-moving and a plausible drama.

4. Guide to the Language and Imagery of *Othello*

Othello was first performed at Court in 1604 and was written probably not much before that time. It was not printed, however, until a quarto edition appeared in 1622. The two principal sources for establishing the text are the 1622 Quarto and the Folio. These sources differ, but both are indispensable. Some modern editors (e.g., M. R. Ridley in the Arden Edition) use the Quarto as the basic text. But most (e.g., J. Dover Wilson and Alice Walker in the New

Cambridge Shakespeare) use the Folio. Whichever of the editions is chosen for the basic text, all editors draw freely upon the other edition to supply important passages.

For the vocabulary of the play, students may use any of the recent excellent editions, most of which have fairly complete notes. Here, under "Language," the endeavor will be to supply information about unusually important words. Curiously and unfortunately, these are not explicated in most editions.

Language: "Epithets of War" and Other Important Words. The major characters in *Othello* are army officers. The jealousy Iago feels for Cassio is in large part, he says, a rivalry for military office. Four of the five acts are set in a "town of war." It is understandable that the military vocabulary in such a play should be of crucial importance. We particularly need to know the meanings and connotations (often very different from modern usage) attaching to the various military titles.

Captain-General Othello. As the foremost officer in the state of Venice and as Governor-General of Cyprus, Othello is clearly a general in rank. He is sometimes, however, referred to as captain. This confusion was not unusual in Elizabethan times, since "captain" was also applied to a general, a survival from Roman times. But there was a more important Elizabethan reason for the confusion. Generals, however exalted their status, usually also kept the proud title of captain of a company. This was their basic and permanent rank. Othello is thus both a captain and a general. He is likewise a mercenary. It was the practice of some Italian city-states to employ a foreigner as head of the army.

Othello possesses all the virtues for a general prescribed by Renaissance military treatises. He is of noble birth; he is self-controlled; he is religious; he has the respect of his men; and he demonstrates the most advanced Renaissance military knowledge in choosing for his lieutenant a man (Cassio) versed in military science rather than one (Iago) who has proved himself only as a good combat soldier. This choice provokes the complaint by Iago in the opening scene, with his contemptuous reference to "the bookish theoric" (I,i, 24).

Lieutenant Cassio and Ancient (i.e., Ensign) Iago. The two ranks of lieutenant and ensign must be considered together, because they were usually so discussed in Renaissance military treatises and because it is the friction between them that resulted in much bitter rivalry in Renaissance armies and in the play of *Othello*.

Although a general was responsible for the wise choice of officers, it was the special function and distinction of a captain to choose good men for his company and to choose, in particular, the lieutenant and ensign so warily that no feuding resulted. Some critics of *Othello* have argued that both Cassio and Iago are field-grade rather than company officers—that their rank would be immediately below that of general. Thus Cassio would really be lieutenant-general and Iago would be (though this rank seems never to haxe existed) ensign to the general. Shakespeare was erratic and sometimes ill-informed in army matters, and there may well have been in this respect something as usefully ambivalent as the "double-time" scheme already discussed. Nevertheless, the relationship between lieutenant and ensign in this play is strikingly parallel to that which we find in the discussion of *company* officers in military treatises. Moreover, a general would be extremely unlikely to "cashier" his lieutenant-general as Othello does Cassio. It is Othello as *captain* who chooses his two officers, lieutenant and ensign, and who discharges one of them.

Ensign was an office of longer standing than that of lieutenant. It was a very honorable rank. Its holder carried the company ensign (or standard), which he was never to desert. In battle if the standard was threatened, all the soldiers had to fight to defend it and its bearer. Thus the ensign had to be universally well liked, brave, and trusted. Iago superlatively meets all three requirements. The rivalry between lieutenant and ensign (suggested in II,iii, 113–114) arose because of the creation of the new and, some thought, unnecessary office of lieutenant.

Honest. This is obviously the most conspicuous word in *Othello.* It is repeatedly applied to Iago, and it is used questioningly in reference to both Desdemona and Cassio. Most glossaries to the play tell us that it meant chaste (a common Elizabethan meaning). A few editors point out also that it sometimes meant honorable or generally virtuous and upright. As applied to Desdemona, it usually did mean chaste; as applied to Cassio, it usually meant honorable. But most often the word is applied to Iago, who makes no pretense to chastity and for whom "honorable" is not usually a sufficiently accurate or rich meaning.

When others call Iago "honest," they mean not simply that he is a virtuous, trustful man, but that he is a plain-spoken critic of knavish types. This is the role that the character Honesty has in the popular anonymous play *A Knack to Know a Knave* (produced in

1592). He has the knack of distinguishing honest men from knaves, and he seeks out and exposes the dishonest. This is the usual meaning of *honest* in the many Character sketches of the Honest Man which appeared at about the time of *Othello*. Thus Honest Iago's reputation is that of one who can detect vice in such persons as Cassio, Desdemona, and Bianca, and who enjoys a liberality of cynical, roughly truthful speech. So viewed, the sobriquet "honest" is applied to Iago with less of the suggestion, usually inferred by critics, of cheap and excessive irony.

Think. This word is used perhaps more often than any other, though its appearances are concentrated in the temptation scene (III,iii). It is distinctively Iago's word, whereas *know* is appropriately Othello's.

Think has not changed appreciably in meaning since Shakespeare's day (though it had then some darker and cruder connotations), but no actor or student can afford to neglect the rich variety of shadings the word is given in the play. No glossary definition would be adequate to convey the range of the drama it conveys (in fact, it is not even listed in glossaries). It varies in intonation and suggestion, as Iago uses it, from intense and painful cerebration to obscene thought which must be kept secret. It is at first a word almost unknown to Othello, who has been accustomed to *know* and to act promptly upon his knowledge. But as Iago, the "thinking man," begins to expose him to uncertainties, Othello assumes this characteristic part of Iago's vocabulary. It is appropriate that he do so, for *thinking* rather than *knowing* is an essential mark of the jealous mind. Iago, who is compact of jealousy, uses the word abundantly throughout the play, but makes most successful use of it during his strategy of the temptation scene. The success of the strategy reaches its climax in Othello's description of his intolerable state of mind:

> By the world,
> I *think* my wife be honest, and *think* she is not;
> I *think* that thou are just, and *think* thou are not.
> I'll have some proof. (III,iii, 383–386)

Hint. This is not an example of a word repeatedly and thematically used. It occurs only twice in the play (I,iii, 142; 166). Upon its correct interpretation, however, depends a considerable bit of evidence for our judging of Othello's character. The relevant episode is this: After Othello—so he tells the senators—had told Desdemona of his hard and romantic life,

> She thank'd me;
> And bade me, if I had a friend that lov'd her,
> I should but teach him how to tell my story,
> And that would woo her. Upon this *hint* I spake.
>   (I,iii, 163–166)

If we interpret *hint* in the modern sense, Othello's statement is an attempt to put half the responsibility for the elopement upon Desdemona in that she provided him a rather obvious "hint" to make his declaration. Such an ungallant action by Othello would seriously lessen our esteem for his integrity (cf. "Not I. I must be found."—I,ii, 30).

G. L. Kittredge, however, has pointed out in his notes to the play that the principal Elizabethan meaning of *hint* was not "a suggestion purposely made," but merely "an occasion," "an opportunity." Such is its meaning in the immediately antecedent usage, also by Othello:

> Wherein of anters vast and deserts idle,
> Rough quarries, rocks, and hills whose heads touch heaven,
> It was my *hint* to speak. . . (I,iii, 140–142)

Thus the correct understanding of a word prevents our seeing Othello as apologetically easing out of a difficulty by blaming it on Desdemona. The most treacherous kind of word which we find in Shakespeare is apt to be not one which we do not recognize, but one which makes sense in its modern meaning.

Imagery. *Imagery,* in its simplest sense, consists of the pictures suggested by words and phrases. In a play the imagery contributes to what Robert B. Heilman has called "verbal" as opposed to "actional" drama.[1] In poetic drama the total impression made upon the audience is sometimes achieved almost as much by imagery as by story. Verbal references to night, to the sea, to gardens, to clothes, and so forth, provide an orchestration for the plain statement of theme. Imagery, as most critics refer to it, consists of more than simile and metaphor. Any kind of image (or picture), whether or not it is metaphorically used, must be taken into account. Nevertheless, in a poetically conceived play, all the figurative language tends to fall into not more than one or two thematically unified subject matters. In *Othello* the main images may be grouped under the following heads: (1) light-and-dark and (2) sea-tempest.

[1] *Magic in the Web* (Lexington, Kentucky: University of Kentucky Press, 1956), pp. 5–6.

Light-and-dark. One of the most arresting features of *Othello*—
that which will at once interest and trouble an audience—is the
marriage of black and white. Even if Shakespeare had not picked up
this theme by imagery, it would still startle an audience. But he did
pick it up. Contrasting light-and-dark imagery throughout the play
testifies to how prominent this motif was in Shakespeare's way of
picturing the drama. This is not, of course, to say that the marriage
of black to white is the most important issue in the play; it assuredly
is not. This contrast becomes reliable as a guide to interpretation
only if we recognize that, as in *Macbeth*, there can be a reversal of
values: that, as the Duke tells Desdemona's grieving father:

> And, noble signior,
> If virtue no delighted beauty lack,
> Your son-in-law is far more fair than black.
> (I,iii, 289–291)

The following quotations are representative of those employing the
light-and-dark imagery:

		Quotation	*Comment*
I,i,	76–77	*As when, by night and negligence, the fire/Is spied in populous cities.*	Much of the play exploits the frightening picture of fire in the night. This image becomes most terrible when Desdemona sees Othello with a burning taper standing by her bed (V,ii).
	88–89	*. . . an old black ram/Is tupping your white ewe.*	Iago characteristically sees the union of dark and light in the grossest way—as the physical union of animals noted for sexuality.
I,iii,	409–410	*Hell and night/Must bring this monstrous birth to the world's light.*	This image aptly pictures Iago's diabolical scheme. Darkness, as well as hell, serves as midwife to bring evil thoughts into the light of consciousness. Night is appropriately the time when most of the evil action takes place.
II,iii,	356–366	*Divinity of hell!/When devils will the blackest sins put on,/They do suggest at first with heavenly shows. . . ./So will I turn her virtue into pitch.*	Iago appears fair in order to do the blackest sins. It is the function of his evil to turn Desdemona's lightness into blackness. This, like the later blackening of Othello's character, is far more serious than the color of skin.

Quotation	*Comment*
III,iii, 386–388 *Her name, that was as fresh/ As Dian's visage, is now be-grim'd and black/As mine own face.*	Through the defiling suggestions of Iago, Othello sees his fair wife so sullied by a blackening obscenity that she seems as black as he is physically.
IV,ii, 71–72 *Was this fair paper, this most goodly book,/Made to write 'whore' upon?*	
V,ii, 3–7 *Yet I'll not shed her blood,/ Nor scar that whiter skin of hers than snow, . . ./Put out the light, and then put out the light.*	Othello enters Desdemona's dark bedchamber carrying a taper. He sees her brightness, which he cannot trust yet hates to sully. Putting out the light suggests the coming of two kinds of darkness for him: (1) night and chaos; (2) the loss of Desdemona and the beauty she embodies. It may also suggest for Othello the extinction of his own integrity.
V,ii, 130–131 *O, the more angel she,/And you the blacker devil!*	Emilia brings home to Othello that his jealousy and crime have made Desdemona even brighter, whereas he has become a "blacker devil."

It is also a part of the progressive spiritual blackening of Othello that he increasingly adopts the coarse animal imagery of Iago. The obscene "Goats and monkeys" which he exclaims (IV,i, 274) represents an incorporation within his own pure nature of the suggestive use made by Iago of goats and monkeys (as lecherous creatures) earlier in the play (III,iii, 403).

Sea-tempest. The Renaissance was much given to using images of the larger world (macrocosm) to reflect the actions of man in the little world (microcosm). One of Shakespeare's favorite macrocosmic images, used most powerfully in *King Lear*, is that of the tempest. In *Othello*, although there is a tremendous storm, the basic image is the sea, with the tempest used secondarily to represent an agitation of the sea. Much of what is happening physically and spiritually to the principal characters is pictured poetically in images of the sea. Montano's question, "What from the cape can you discern at sea?" (II,i, 1), is a thematic statement of the sea imagery in the play.

Iago, a prosaic, plain-spoken person, uses nautical images as would a professional sailor.[1] He is "belee'd and calm'd" (I,i, 30). He sees Othello's successful courtship of Desdemona in terms of

[1] See Caroline F. E. Spurgeon, *Shakespeare's Imagery* (New York: The Macmillan Company; Cambridge, England: At the University Press, 1935), p. 337.

piratical pillage: "Faith, he to-night hath boarded a land carack" (I,ii, 50). And the prospering of his wicked scheme is pictured in terms of a vessel being aided by winds and currents:

> If consequence do but approve my dream,
> My boat sails freely, both with wind and stream.
> (II,iii, 64–65)

There is nothing romantic or picturesque about Iago's utilitarian view of the sea. It has no tempests for him: no danger and no beauty.

The other main characters are more poetically involved in the symbolism of the sea, and what happens to their lives and fortunes is foreboded or paralleled by what happens through the agitation of the sea. The life voyage of Othello, in particular, can be traced through the imagery of sea and tempest; but it is worth noting what the sea does to, and what it has to tell us about, all the principal characters.

		Quotation	Comment
II,i,	12–17	*The chidden billow seems to pelt the clouds;/ . . . I never did like molestation view/On the enchafed flood.*	The storm has an ominous suggestiveness and an almost supernatural violence.
	21–22	*The desparate tempest hath so bang'd the Turks/That their designment halts.*	The storm is not altogether malevolent for Othello. It has ended one war for him, though it will serve to forebode another kind of strife.
	44–46	*O, let the heavens/Give him [Othello] defence against the elements,/For I have lost him on a dangerous sea!*	Ironic premonition, for Cassio will shortly lose Othello in a more painful sense.
	92–93	*The great contention of the sea and skies/Parted our fellowship.*	
	48–49	*His [Othello's] bark is stoutly timber'd, and his pilot/Of very expert and approv'd allowance.*	This is a preview, in nautical terms, of the struggle Othello will have ashore and of his strong character in facing it. But the optimism about the "pilot" is sadly inapplicable to the kind of guidance he will have in his most desperate need.
	66–67	*'Tis one Iago, ancient to the General./Has had most favourable and happy speed.*	The tempest (like the rain falling on the just and the unjust) permits Iago to pass through swiftly to the island

Quotation	*Comment*
	where he will create disaster in many lives.
68–73 *Tempests themselves, high seas, and howling winds . . . /As having sense of beauty, do omit/Their mortal natures, letting go safely by/The divine Desdemona.*	Once again the tempest is not totally malevolent. It lets Desdemona safely through, as she will go safely through—in a spiritual sense—her ensuing tempest on the island.
77–78 *Great Jove, Othello guard,/And swell his sail with thine own pow'rful breath.*	Cassio prays for his general's safe passage through the tempest at sea.
186–191 *O my soul's joy!/If after every tempest come such calms,/May the winds blow till they have waken'd death!/And let the labouring bark climb hills of seas/Olympus-high, and duck again as low/As hell's from heaven!*	Othello can fully express his joy at the sight of Desdemona only through images of the sea which he knows so well. Note the difference between the ardor of his sea imagery and the flatness of Iago's. The speech is important also as pointing to the reunion and calm that usually follow a storm in Shakespeare. Here there is irony, for the reunion and calm will be short-lived.
III,iii, 453–460 *Never, Iago. Like to the Pontic sea,/Whose icy current and compulsive course/Ne'er feels retiring ebb, but keeps due on/To the Propontic and the Hellespont;/Even so my bloody thoughts, with violent pace,/Shall ne'er look back, ne'er ebb to humble love,/Till that a capable and wide revenge/Swallow them up.*	The relentless "icy current" of Othello's "bloody thoughts" marks the turning-point of the play. Othello could not have chosen a better image to express the finality of his change from love to hate. The tempest, so often referred to in II,i, is now replaced by an even grimmer symbol of Othello's fatal voyage, "my bloody thoughts."
V,ii, 267–268 *Here is my journey's end, here is my butt,/And very seamark of my utmost sail.*	In recognizing his total calamity and approaching death, Othello sees it all as the end of a sea voyage. Both the tempest and the icy currents, with their beautiful yet terrible agitation, are now gone.

We have here looked only at the two dominant kinds of imagery in the play. The reader interested in a full study of the imagery will profit from Robert B. Heilman's tracing of all kinds of image strands, including images of birth, burning, clothing, pain and torture, medicine, economics, and poison. Wolfgang Clemen is also discerning in his study of the ways in which Othello and Iago are contrasted by their characteristic choice of images.

5. Characters: Analysis of Their Qualities and Development

Drama presents people in action. How they think, speak, act, and interact makes a play. The following analyses will assist the reader in becoming better acquainted with the principal characters in *Othello*, and in following their development as a result of the action.

OTHELLO

Love for Desdemona	Quotation	Comment
I,iii, 167–168	*She lov'd me for the dangers I had pass'd,/And I lov'd her that she did pity them.*	Robert B. Heilman, among others, considers that this statement shows a lack of completeness in Othello's love for Desdemona. It perhaps does not indicate a secure ground for a mature love.
I,iii, 299–301	*Come, Desdemona. I have but an hour/Of love, of worldly matters and direction,/To spend with thee. We must obey the time.*	G. R. Elliott, who finds excessive pride in Othello, considers this a patronizing speech, indicating Othello's somewhat contemptuous attitude toward love. It may thus be a sort of self-deception, because Othello soon must learn exactly how important his love is. The speech might be considered typical of a warrior who has not been in love before.
II,i, 186–187	*O my soul's joy!/If after every tempest come such calms, . . .*	This passage shows both the ardor and potential violence of Othello's love.
II,i, 191–192	*If it were now to die,/'Twere now to be most happy; . . .*	This speech is beautiful and heartfelt, and shows that Othello's love for Desdemona, if not perfect, is indeed deep and sincere. The death image has ironic overtones, however.
II,iii, 349–354	*. . . were't to renounce his baptism—/All seals and symbols of redeemed sin—/His soul is so enfetter'd to her love/That she may make, unmake, do what she list,/Even as her appetite shall play the god/With his weak function.*	The love that causes Othello to exclaim "I will deny thee nothing" is here turned to weakness by a contemptuous Iago.

Love for Desdemona	Quotation	Comment
III,iii, 55–76	*Not now, sweet Desdemon; . . . The sooner, sweet, for you. . . . I will deny thee nothing.*	Some critics think he is playing with her here, but there is little of the playful about Othello.
III,iii, 90–92	*Excellent wretch! Perdition catch my soul/But I do love thee! and when I love thee not,/Chaos is come again.*	An ironic speech, full of portent, for order and calm in Othello's limited military life, only lately broadened by his marriage, depend upon his assurance of love for Desdemona.

Romantic Idealism		
I,iii, 171	*I think this tale would win my daughter too.*	There is an evident appeal in Othello's innocence and romantic background. Even the naïveté of the courtship is winning.
III,iv, 46–47	*A liberal hand! The hearts of old gave hands;/But our new heraldry is hands, not hearts.*	Perhaps it is his pain at a destroyed ideal which makes him play so cruelly with Desdemona.
IV,i, 35–44	*Lie with her? lie on her? . . . It is not words that shakes me thus.—Pish! Noses, ears, and lips? . . . Confess? —handkerchief?—O devil!*	Here his imagination runs riot, and he falls into a fit. The sexual side of marriage, vividly conveyed to him by Iago, profoundly disturbs him. His view of love is to see Desdemona as a "fair warrior" and one who pities him.
IV, i, 198–207	*So delicate with a needle! . . . Of so high and plenteous wit and invention! . . . But yet the pity of it, Iago! O Iago, the pity of it, Iago!*	Othello's saving grace is his ability in the midst of his passion to feel the sorrow of a perfect being so corrupted.
IV,ii, 35–68	*Come, swear it, damn thyself; . . . Swear thou art honest. . . . O thou weed,/ Who art so lovely fair, and smell'st so sweet, . . .*	The contrast between her beauty and her evil is almost unbearable to a man who trusts in what seems to be true.
V,ii, 1–22	*It is the cause, it is the cause, my soul. . . . Yet I'll not shed her blood, . . . Yet she must die, else she'll betray more men. . . . and I will kill thee, /And love thee after. . . . This sorrow's heavenly;/It strikes where it doth love.*	The same idealism which colors his love and his jealousy, and is the cause of some of his self-deception, turns the murder from passion into a ritual purge. He at last realizes that it is not simple to cast off love; nevertheless he still does not understand his own motivation for the murder.

Trustfulness	Quotation	Comment
I,iii, 284–286	*. . . my ancient./A man he is of honesty and trust./To his conveyance I assign my wife, . . .*	Othello has no reason to distrust Iago at this point; it is evident that he also trusts his wife, since he assigns her to the care of another man. The lack of a hint of sexual jealousy here makes Othello's later breakdown the more striking.
I,iii, 294–296	*She has deceiv'd her father, and may thee./My life upon her faith!—Honest Iago,/My Desdemona must I leave to thee.*	Brabantio suggests one of the ideas later used by Iago to undermine Othello's trust. Othello's reply is significant, for his life is forfeit upon his loss of faith in her; faith in Desdemona becomes a requisite of his life and sanity.
I,iii, 405–406	*The Moor is of a free and open nature/That thinks men honest that but seem to be so; . . .*	Iago's words about Othello are not always to be trusted, but here he characterizes his victim admirably. Othello he knows to be unsuspicious, neither introspective nor possessed of much insight into the motivations of others. (Cf. *Innocence*)
III,iii, 258–260	*This fellow's of exceeding honesty,/And knows all qualities, with a learned spirit/Of human dealings.*	Othello is inclined to trust Iago; Iago is a man, and Othello is used to dealing with men. Iago, moreover, has a reputation for honesty. Othello demonstrates again his need to trust people, his inability to deal with dissembling, which makes his agony in choosing between Iago and his wife the greater.
III,iii, 278–279	*If she be false, O, then heaven mocks itself!/I'll not believe't.*	Othello demonstrates his extreme need to trust his wife, as in other speeches he indicates his need to trust Iago. Because there is as yet no evil in himself, he has no basis, no "jealousy," for seeing it in others.
III,iii, 325	*The Moor already changes with my poison.*	Othello's inclination to trust Iago is, of course, easily perceived by Iago. The poison-jealousy image is developed by "Dr. Iago."
V,i, 31–32	*O brave Iago, honest and just, /Thou hast such noble sense of thy friend's wrong!*	In the breakdown of his ordered existence Othello desperately clings to the one thing

Trustfulness	*Quotation*	*Comment*
		which seems certain—Iago's friendship.

Self-deception

I,iii, 230–234	*The tyrant custom . . . Hath made the flinty and steel couch of war/My thrice-driven bed of down. I do agnize/A natural and prompt alacrity/I find in hardness; . . .*	This might have been uttered by a confirmed bachelor; the alacrity with which he undertakes the war makes marriage seem unnatural. One wonders if he is deceived about his desire for marriage.
I,iii, 262–266	*I . . . beg it not/To please the palate of my appetite,/Nor to comply with heat . . . But to be free and bounteous to her mind.*	Here it seems impossible for him to be passion's slave. But, according to Elliott, this is anticlimactic after Desdemona's plea (her speech was pure—his, sexual). He speaks as one loving his pride. There is a proud self-deception at work in Othello's character.
I,iii, 278–279	*You must hence to-night. . . . With all my heart.*	He is still, according to some critics, playing a role which he cannot maintain—he is being passionless, the good soldier who puts personal matters aside for the sake of duty. "Othello's occupation's gone" he cries (III,iii, 357) when he finds himself involved in personal matters.
II,iii, 1–3	*. . . look you to the guard tonight./Let's teach ourselves that honourable stop,/Not to outsport discretion.*	Here he seems to be well aware that the revels may bring forth quarrels and indiscretion. In view of this, his outburst after the fight seems peculiar.
III,iii, 190–192	*I'll see before I doubt; when I doubt, prove;/And on the proof there is no more but this—/Away at once with love or jealousy!*	Othello will find it is not so easy as he thinks to make a choice between love and jealousy and dispel that not chosen. His love for Desdemona continues and creates a new deception, the ritualistic murder.

Innocence (Simplicity)

I,iii, 81–87	*Rude am I in my speech,/And little bless'd with the soft*	Heilman, who sees Othello's confidence in himself as a kind

Innocence (Simplicity)		Quotation	Comment
		phrase of peace; . . . And little of this great world can I speak/More than pertains to feats of broil and battle; . . .	of naive complacency, considers this the one area in which Othello will acknowledge his inferiority. Here he maintains his self-assurance; later he is less secure (III,iii, 264).
I,iii,	90	*I will a round unvarnish'd tale deliver . . .*	Othello's most appealing quality is observable in this speech; but there is no feeling of shame in his confession of simplicity.
I,iii,	128–169	*Her father lov'd me . . . Still question'd me the story of my life . . . This to hear/Would Desdemona seriously incline; . . . This only is the witch-craft I have us'd.*	There is a touching innocence in his belief that it was the spell of his tales alone which won Desdemona.
I,iii,	156–158	*And often did beguile her of her tears/When I did speak of some distressful stroke/That my youth suffer'd.*	Desdemona had found a perpetual youth and innocence in this middle-aged man. "He is not selfish though self-centered; naively, moderately, proud of his career; devoid of pity for himself but eliciting all of hers" (Elliott).
II,i,	206–207	*Honey, you shall be well de-sir'd in Cyprus;/I have found great love amongst them.*	This prating may be an indication of immaturity, if one insists, as do some critics, upon finding Othello largely responsible for his tragedy.
II,i,	224–225	*Mark me with what violence she first lov'd the Moor, but for bragging and telling her fantastical lies; . . .*	Iago, as usual, casts a cold, cynical eye upon the Moor's tales, making him appear a fool for telling them and for believing Desdemona influenced by them.
III,iii,	339–347	*I saw't not, thought it not, it harm'd not me. . . . I had been happy if the general camp, . . . had tasted her sweet body,/So I had nothing known.*	Here Othello states clearly the dilemma of the nonthinking man forced into a position where he must ponder and speculate.
III,iii,	384–386	*I think my wife be honest, and think she is not;/I think that thou art just, and think thou art not./I'll have some proof.*	His innocence is gone. He must think, since he knows not how to believe. This is painful; but it does not seem to lead, as in *King Lear,* to the firm wisdom of self-knowledge.

Soldierly Courage	Quotation	Comment
I,iii, 47–49	*Here comes Brabantio and the valiant Moor./Valiant Othello, we must straight employ you/ Against the general enemy Ottoman.*	This is the first of a series of comments by other characters attesting Othello's courage and ability as a warrior.
I,iii, 83–85	*. . . since these arms of mine had seven years' pith . . . they have us'd/Their dearest action in the tented field; . . .*	He has been a soldier since he was seven years old. The life and customs of the soldier are what he is used to, and to him war is a proud and glorious way of life.
II,i, 27–38	*. . . the warlike Moor Othello, . . . For I have serv'd him, and the man commands/Like a full soldier. . . . brave Othello, . . .*	Another comment upon Othello's courage as a soldier, coming from a professional.
III,iv, 134–137	*Can he be angry? I have seen the cannon/When it hath blown his ranks into the air/ And, like the devil, from his very arm/Puff'd his own brother—*	Even in the most provocative military situations, Othello had controlled his anger. Iago professes surprise and incredulity that his general should be less in command now.

Blackness (Exoticism)		
I,ii, 62–75	*O thou foul thief, . . . thou hast practis'd on her with foul charms,/Abus'd her delicate youth with drugs or minerals /That weaken motion.*	Brabantio presents the first of a series of references to Othello's color which emphasize the exotic nature of his marriage with Desdemona. Here Brabantio suggests that unnatural means must have been used to win her.
I,iii, 98	*To fall in love with what she fear'd to look on!*	Brabantio, like Iago, considers there to be something fearful, as well as something disturbingly alien, in Othello's blackness.
I,iii, 290–291	*If virtue no delighted beauty lack,/Your son-in-law is far more fair than black.*	The light-and-dark motif of the play is here used in its moral sense. The Duke contrasts Othello's black exterior with the purity and goodness of his soul.
II,i, 228–234	*Her eye must be fed; and what delight shall she have to look on the devil? . . . loveliness in favour, sympathy in years, manners, and beauties; all which the Moor is defective in.*	Iago represents the spirit of cynicism. He cannot see in Othello's blackness, age, and foreign birth more than an impediment to lust.

Blackness (Exoticism)	Quotation	Comment
III,iii, 386–388	*Her name, that was as fresh /As Dian's visage, is now be- grim'd and black/As mine own face.*	This is taken by most critics as evidence that Othello is black. Also, the passage de- velops the light-and-dark imagery, showing how corrup- tion within Othello's soul makes even dark a symbol of purity.
Dignity (Self- control)		
I,ii, 17–19	*Let him do his spite./My services which I have done the signiory/Shall outtongue his complaints.*	Othello refuses to be alarmed by Iago's account of the wrath of Brabantio. He knows, modestly but surely, his worth.
I,ii, 30–32	*I must be found./My parts, my title, and my perfect soul/ Shall manifest me rightly.*	He will not retreat before Brabantio's men. At this stage of the play he has not tasted Iago's "poison," which will make him distrustful of him- self and of others.
I,ii, 59–61	*Keep up your bright swords, for the dew will rust them./ Good signior, you shall more command with years/Than with your weapons.*	Othello remains calm in the face of Brabantio's swords- men, and gracious to his father-in-law. His perfect con- fidence in himself makes others look small beside him.
I,iii, 76	*Most potent, grave, and rev- erend signiors, . . .*	His answer to Brabantio's charge of witchcraft is ad- mirably restrained, in con- trast with Brabantio's hys- teria.
III,iii, 359–360	*Villain, be sure thou prove my love a whore!/Be sure of it; give me the ocular proof; . . .*	Some actors have seized their Iagos by the throat at this speech. It indicates the break- down of Othello's self-control.
III,iii, 445–451	*All my fond love thus do I blow to heaven. . . . Arise, black vengeance, . . . O, blood, blood, blood!*	Lodovico makes the definitive comment upon this change in Othello: "Is this the nature/ Whom passion could not shake?" (IV,i, 276–277)
III,iv, 26–28	*. . . my noble Moor/Is true of mind, and made of no such baseness/As jealous creatures are, . . .*	Desdemona is judging the character of the Othello she knew.
IV,i, 276–279	*Is this the nature/Whom pas- sion could not shake? whose solid virtue/The shot of acci- dent nor dart of chance/*	Lodovico, struck with wonder at the change in Othello, his seizures, his jealous ravings, describes the character of the

Dignity (Self-control)	Quotation	Comment
	Could neither graze nor pierce?	Othello he knew.
Passion (Imagination)		
II,iii, 204–207	*Now, by heaven,/My blood begins my safer guides to rule,/And passion, having my best judgment collied,/Assays to lead the way.*	An extremely significant speech, for it shows the depths of emotion Othello has heretofore held in check. Lacking introspective tendencies, Othello is unable to make a rational assessment of his emotional potency.
II,iii, 207–210	*If I once stir/Or do but lift this arm, the best of you/Shall sink in my rebuke.*	His assurance has deserted him at this threat to his authority, and he reacts in a manner described variously as barbaric, primitive, or immature.
III,iii, 105–116	*What dost thou think? . . . By heaven, he echoes me,/As if there were some monster in his thought . . . If thou dost love me,/Show me thy thought.*	Some critics consider Othello to be too ready to seize upon a pretext for jealousy. There is, however, great power in Iago's sly hints; they strike at a basic inability of Othello to deal with ambiguities, nuances, and disorders.
III,iii, 239–240	*If more thou dost perceive, let me know more./Set on thy wife to observe.*	His nobility gone, Othello has descended to employing spies against his wife. This represents the beginning of the humiliation and degradation of soul which accompany his jealousy. His tendency is to trust "honest Iago."
III,iii, 347–357	*O, now for ever/Farewell the tranquil mind! farewell content! . . . Pride, pomp, and circumstance of glorious war! . . . Farewell! Othello's occupation's gone!*	At last the extent to which his life is bound up in his love is brought home to Othello. Gone is the casual attitude which made him dismiss Desdemona and turn eagerly to war.
III,iii, 460–462	*Now, by yond marble heaven,/In the due reverence of a sacred vow/I here engage my words.*	Othello is a poet in his great distress. His imagination runs riot (cf. his exoticism).
V,ii, 97–100	*My wife! my wife! what wife? I have no wife. . . . O heavy hour!/Methinks it should be now a huge eclipse/Of sun and moon, . . .*	Again his great sorrow turns to great poetry, and his chaos is indeed come again.

IAGO

Reputation		*Quotation*	*Comment*
I,i,	115–118	*What profane wretch art thou? . . . Thou art a villain.*	Brabantio, enraged by Iago's coarse language, inadvertently speaks truth about the ancient. No one else at this point, except Iago himself, says anything damaging to Iago's reputation.
I,iii,	284–285	*. . . my ancient./A man he is of honesty and trust.*	Iago's reputation for a good-hearted, soldierly honesty, to which deceitfulness is foreign, is a major cause of his control over Othello later in the play.
I,iii,	295–296	*Honest Iago,/My Desdemona must I leave to thee.*	Some critics think this is a rather casual handing over of Desdemona, but there is probably no undervaluing of Desdemona in the speech, and it does indicate the depth of trust Othello places in Iago.
II,iii,	177–178	*Honest Iago, that looks dead with grieving,/Speak. Who began this? On thy love, I charge thee.*	Iago has established himself as one of the few trustworthy people in a world of dissemblers. Othello turns to him at once for an explanation of the fight.
II,iii,	315–341	*. . . good Lieutenant, I think you think I love you. . . . You advise me well. . . . Good night, honest Iago.*	Othello is not the only one capable of falling under Iago's spell. Cassio grows more convinced of Iago's honesty and helpfulness as this scene progresses.
III,iii,	5	*. . . that's an honest fellow.*	Even Desdemona concurs in the prevailing opinion of Iago, as does his wife.
III,iii	118–119	*And, for I know thou'rt full of love and honesty/And weigh'st thy words before thou giv'st them breath, . . .*	Othello indicates Iago's reputation for thoughtfulness as well as honesty.
III,iii,	258–260	*This fellow's of exceeding honesty,/And knows all qualities, with a learned spirit/Of human dealings.*	Iago has shaken Othello's faith in humanity, and Othello is reassuring himself of Iago's honesty. Here it becomes apparent the extent to which Iago's success depends upon his reputation. Note that, here and elsewhere, *honesty* implies a critical, searching spirit as well as rectitude.
IV,ii,	130–134	*I will be hang'd if some eternal villain,/Some busy and in-*	Again the truth is told by one (Emilia) who never suspects

Reputation		Quotation	Comment
		sinuating rogue, . . . Have not devis'd this slander. . . . Fie, there is no such man!	that her words have found their mark. Iago jumps swiftly to a denial, indicating a rather human nervousness about the success of his plan—not any real alarm at the recognition of his true nature.
V,i,	31–33	*O brave Iago, honest and just,/That hast such noble sense of thy friend's wrong!/ Thou teachest me.*	This is Othello's great statement of a faith in Iago which has never really wavered.
V,i,	52	*. . . a very valiant fellow.*	Lodovico praises the ancient for a quality, totally unearned, with which everyone seems to credit him.
V,ii,	242–243	*I'll after that same villain,/ For 'tis a damned slave.*	A significant final comment upon Iago. His "reputation" is finally that of merely a "villain," "a damned slave."

Bluntness
(Soldierly
Heartiness)

I,ii,	1–4	*Though in the trade of war I have slain men,/Yet do I hold it very stuff o'th' conscience/To do no contriv'd murther. I lack iniquity/ Sometimes to do me service.*	For Othello's benefit Iago takes the pose of the rough and ready but good-hearted soldier.
I,ii,	4–5	*Nine or ten times/I had thought t' have yerk'd him here under the ribs.*	Iago is the man of action who would appeal to a professional soldier like Othello. This sort of expression enhances his reputation for honesty.
II,i,	166–167	*You may relish him more in the soldier than in the scholar.*	A plain-speaking soldier is how he appears to Cassio.
II,iii,	70–71	*Some wine, ho!/And let me the canakin clink, clink; . . .*	Iago can be a genial, rough, good fellow to serve his purpose.
II,iii,	220–247	*Touch me not so near./I had rather have this tongue cut from my mouth/Than it should do offence to Michael Cassio. . . . I know, Iago,/ Thy honesty and love doth mince this matter, . . .*	Iago uses strong, bluff language, devoid of subtlety, and to all appearances full of honest sorrow.
II,iii,	301	*Come, you are too severe a moraler.*	Hearty good will fairly drips from Iago as he counsels Cassio.
III,iii,	126–127	*Men should be what they seem;/ Or those that be not, would they might seem none!*	He seems straightforward in this speech, which is probably accompanied by a worried frown. It is this sort of speech

Bluntness (Soldierly Heartiness)	Quotation	Comment
		which makes Iago's seeming evasiveness the more tormenting to Othello in the temptation scene.
IV,i, 287–289	*Alas, alas!/It is not honesty in me to speak/What I have seen and known.*	Iago is capable of putting on a similar act with Lodovico. In short, his accomplished straightforwardness wins each character in his turn.

Guile (Duplicity)		
I,i, 42	*I follow him to serve my turn upon him.*	There is a suggestion of the "damned slave" in this confession of purpose.
I,i, 57–65	*Were I the Moor, I would not be Iago./In following him, I follow but myself; . . . I am not what I am.*	At certain points throughout the play Iago unmasks himself and allows us to glimpse the cleverness of his seeming. Roderigo should heed this warning, but instead is reassured by it.
I,iii, 398–402	*Cassio's a proper man. . . . After some time to abuse Othello's ear/That he is too familiar with his wife.*	Here we see the arch-villain at plotting, casting his characters for their roles in an "amateur" tragedy of his own, almost extemporaneous, authorship.
II,iii, 16–18	*He hath not yet made wanton the night with her, and she is sport for Jove. . . . a most exquisite lady.*	Cassio is not betrayed into making a disrespectful remark about Desdemona.
II,iii, 268–270	*Reputation is an idle and most false imposition; oft got without merit and lost without deserving.*	Iago's words to Cassio are ironic in the light of Iago's own reputation; they indicate how accomplished Iago is at saying what others would like to hear.
II,iii, 342–343	*And what's he then that says I play the villain,/When this advice is free I give and honest, . . .*	Iago indulges himself in a little gloating at the success of his cozening. His intelligence glories in the contrast between apparent good and real evil.
III,iii, 152–154	*It were not for your quiet nor your good,/Nor for my manhood, honesty, or wisdom,/To let you know my thoughts.*	This scene shows Iago's guile working to greatest effect.
III,iii, 155–156	*Good name in man and woman, dear my lord,/Is the immediate jewel of their souls.*	Again it is ironic that Iago uses the truth upon which the success of his plan depends to further that plan.

Guile (Duplicity)	Quotation	Comment
III,iii, 202–203	*In Venice they do let heaven see the pranks/They dare not show their husbands; . . .*	Iago obviously plays upon Othello's ignorance of Venice. He suggests that Venetian women are accustomed to adultery—something of which Othello, a stranger, could not be aware.
III,iii, 214–220	*I see this hath a little dash'd your spirits. . . . I am to pray you not to strain my speech . . . to larger reach/ Than to suspicion.*	As this entire scene shows, Iago always knows the proper remark to increase Othello's suspicion without giving the impression that he wishes to do so.
III,iii, 375–377	*O wretched fool,/That liv'st to make thine honesty a vice!/ O monstrous world!*	Iago skillfully berates himself for his fond honesty.
IV,i, 79–101	*Cassio came hither. . . . Do but encave yourself/And mark the fleers, the gibes, and notable scorns . . . Now will I question Cassio of Bianca, . . . As he shall smile, Othello shall go mad.*	A clever trick, but not of Iago's usual subtlety.

Jealousy

I,i, 8–11	*Three great ones of the city,/ In personal suit to make me his lieutenant,/Off-capp'd to him; and, by the faith of man, /I know my price, I am worth no worse a place.*	Iago's malice is in part due to jealousy over Othello's preference for other officers in promotion. But the next quotation indicates that Iago has more than one ground—indeed too many grounds—for credibly motivated jealousy.
I,iii, 392–394	*I hate the Moor;/And it is thought abroad that 'twixt my sheets/'Has done my office. I know not if't be true; . . .*	Emilia also mentions the sexual jealousy which grips Iago. ("Some such squire . . . made you to suspect me with the Moor"—IV,ii, 145–147.)
II,i, 168–169	*He takes her by the palm. Ay, well said, whisper!*	Iago sees subtle meanings which even Roderigo knows are not there.
II,i, 257–258	*If she had been blessed, she would never have lov'd the Moor.*	Iago understands people very well when he needs to manipulate them (cf. *Guile*), but he does not understand their motivation.
II,i, 295–316	*That Cassio loves her, I do well believe it; . . . (For I fear Cassio with my nightcap too)*	A third motive intrudes, and Iago succeeds in convincing himself that Desdemona does love Cassio and therefore he must hate Cassio.
V,i, 18–20	*If Cassio do remain,/He hath a daily beauty in his life/ That makes me ugly; . . .*	The daily beauty is in part the love which Iago has

Jealousy		Quotation	Comment
			manufactured between Cassio and Desdemona. In part it is Cassio's gentility. But mainly Iago's view is colored by his paranoid reaction to other people. He is almost insanely troubled by the virtues of others, especially since he cannot understand them.

Cynicism

I,i,	42–45	*I follow him to serve my turn upon him. . . . You shall mark/Many a duteous and knee-crooking knave. . . .*	Iago sneers at duty and loyalty. He considers himself beyond trivial morality; and in fact he is, for he is incapable of feeling it.
I,iii,	313–318	*. . . and since I could distinguish betwixt a benefit and an injury, I never found man that knew how to love himself. Ere I would say I would drown myself for the love of a guinea hen, I would change my humanity with a baboon.*	Iago's self-esteem is maintained with difficulty, for he is basically cynical; yet he can offer other people conventional advice on how to value themselves. Even the encouragement here offered to Roderigo involves a cynicism toward love for others.
I,iii,	348–352	*It cannot be that Desdemona should long continue her love to the Moor— . . . nor he his to her. It was a violent commencement, and thou shalt see an answerable sequestration.*	Iago may be partly right; but because of his criminal strategy, we are never given a chance to see how well or how long Othello's marriage would normally prosper.
I,iii,	389–392	*Thus do I ever make my fool my purse;/For I mine own gain'd knowledge should profane/If I would time expend with such a snipe/But for my sport and profit.*	Rightly he is disdainful of Roderigo's stupidity. He is, however, willing to make use of it.
II,i,	120	*For I am nothing if not critical.*	Iago often speaks the truth about himself. In the passage which follows he gives a demonstration of this characteristic.
II,i,	130	*If she be fair and wise, . . .*	Iago's contempt for sycophants extends to detraction of all good. This speech, though spoken playfully, indicates the depth of his distortion.
II,i,	149–161	*She that was ever fair, and never proud; . . . She was a wight (if ever such wight were)— . . . To suckle fools*	Desdemona perceives the lack of substance behind this sort of judgment ("O most lame and impotent conclusion");

Cynicism	Quotation	Comment
	and chronicle small beer.	but his cynical comments about women, however sincerely he may hold them, he expresses with a disarming wit and playfulness.
II,i, 224–226	*Mark me with what violence she first lov'd the Moor, but for bragging and telling her fantastical lies; . . .*	Some critics feel that Iago's contempt for Othello's wooing is justified. However, Iago fails to understand the nature of the attachment, and sees its success in Othello's terms —not in Desdemona's. (Cf. "I saw Othello's visage in his mind" I,iii, 253.)
III,iii, 146–148	*(As I confess it is my nature's plague/To spy into abuses, and oft my jealousy/Shapes faults that are not), . . .*	Iago's cynicism appears again in the guise of an overly zealous concern for Othello's welfare.

*Intelligence
(Wit)*

I,i, 49–50	*Others there are/Who, trimm'd in forms and visages of duty, . . .*	Iago is capable of perceiving the difference between the real and the apparent when the apparent is good and the real is evil. He has more trouble with Desdemona, who is as good as she seems.
I,i, 59–65	*. . . not I for love and duty, /But seeming so, for my peculiar end; . . . But I will wear my heart upon my sleeve/For daws to peck at.*	The perversion of Iago's intelligence is well indicated here, the callousness which will be the basis of his machinations, the amorality which allows him to do his evil.
I,iii, 322–335	*Virtue? a fig! 'Tis in ourselves that we are thus or thus. . . . If the balance of our lives had not one scale of reason to poise another of sensuality, the blood and baseness of our natures would conduct us to most prepost-'rous conclusions. But we have reason to cool our raging motions, . . .*	Iago can be the moral philosopher when it serves his purpose. But Elizabethan appreciation of the wisdom of this speech would have been tempered by the awareness that it was a stale commonplace. It does not come from Iago's own thought-processes and it tells us nothing about his real convictions. He is like a man skillfully reciting a speech he does not understand.
II,i, 101–103	*Sir, would she give you so much of her lips/As of her tongue she oft bestows on me, /You would have enough.*	This is the wit which makes Iago both a comic character and engaging to others. One must not forget that, beneath the smile, there is a fanatical

Intelligence (Wit)	Quotation	Comment
		jealousy of the man who is kissing his wife.
II,i, 110–116	*You are pictures out of doors, . . . and housewives in your beds. . . . Nay, it is true, or else I am a Turk./You rise to play, and go to bed to work.*	Iago's jovial wit is working playfully here; elsewhere, however, we can see that his profane view of women, his nearly psychotic conviction of their invariable lust, is deeply held.
IV,ii, 207–216	*Why, now I see there's mettle in thee; . . . your suspicion is not without wit and judgment.*	Iago's contempt for Roderigo expresses itself in ironic praise. He enjoys, as only an egotist can, the coarse artistry of sarcasm.
V,ii, 303–304	*Demand me nothing. What you know, you know./From this time forth I never will speak word.*	His perceptions now indicate that this is the best course of action. His intelligence, when confronted with his defeat, turns sullen; perhaps his wit cannot operate.

Sensuality

I,i, 68–71	*Make after him, poison his delight,/Proclaim him in the streets. Incense her kinsmen,/ And though he in a fertile climate dwell,/Plague him with flies; . . .*	Iago's language is often bawdy and coarse, indicating a certain blindness to all but the grosser emotions.
I,i, 87–89	*Your heart is burst; you have lost half your soul./Even now, now, very now, an old black ram/Is tupping your white ewe.*	Iago's language effectively awakens Brabantio; it also indicates his preoccupation with the animalistic side of marriage and the prurient delight which he takes in the mating of black and white.
II,i, 224–238	*Mark me with what violence she first lov'd the Moor, . . . her delicate tenderness will find itself abus'd, begin to heave the gorge, disrelish and abhor the Moor.*	Iago sees only the sexual side of the marriage, failing to perceive the real attraction between Desdemona and Othello.
III,iii, 395–398	*Would you, . . . Behold her topp'd? . . . It were a tedious difficulty, I think,/To bring them to that prospect.*	Iago knows when to introduce the cruder words for the thing he is accusing Desdemona of. Earlier, these words would merely have angered Othello; now they excite in him the form of lust which is a part of the worst stage of jealousy.

DESDEMONA

Love (Devotion)	Quotation	Comment
I,iii, 145–150	*This to hear/Would Desdemona seriously incline; . . . and with a greedy ear/Devour up my discourse.*	This unusual courtship mirrors the unusual nature of Desdemona's love.
I,iii, 167	*She lov'd me for the dangers I had pass'd, . . .*	There is a suggestion of girlish romance in this reason for love; but it complements Desdemona's own strength.
I,iii, 251–252	*My heart's subdu'd/Even to the very quality of my lord.*	This statement shows more maturity in her love than would be indicated by Othello's comment above (I, iii, 167).
I,iii, 253–260	*I saw Othello's visage in his mind,/And to his honours and his valiant parts/Did I my soul and fortunes consecrate. . . . Let me go with him.*	There is more than hero-worship in this love. Desdemona has made a significant choice and understands its implications for her future.
IV,ii, 159–161	*Unkindness may do much;/And his unkindness may defeat my life,/But never taint my love.*	
IV,iii, 19–21	*My love doth so approve him /That even his stubbornness, his checks, his frowns . . . have grace and favour in them.*	It is an ominous, though engaging, aspect of Desdemona's love that it is not to be affected by brutal treatment.
Courage (Strength)		
I,iii, 159–163	*She gave me for my pains a world of sighs. . . . swore . . . 'twas strange . . . 'Twas pitiful . . . she wish'd/That heaven had made her such a man.*	It is the man's strength she admires and wishes for, though her own delicate strength will soon be proved.
I,iii, 181–189	*I do perceive here a divided duty. . . . But here's my husband;/And so much duty . . . I challenge that I may profess /Due to the Moor my lord.*	This is the first demonstration of her courage.
I,iii, 249–251	*That I did love the Moor to live with him,/My downright violence, and storm of fortunes,/May trumpet to the world.*	Desdemona is well aware of what her choice has meant. It will entail hardship and perhaps social criticism. It is unlikely, however, that she has any premonition that her "storm of fortunes" will take the form of violence to her from the man she loves.

Courage (Strength)	Quotation	Comment
II,i, 123–124	*I am not merry; but I do beguile/The thing I am by seeming otherwise.*	Although worried about Othello, she can carry on a bantering conversation with Iago.
II,i, 184	*O my fair warrior!*	According to many critics, this statement indicates Othello's awareness of the courage which Desdemona displays.
III,iii, 68–83	*I wonder in my soul/What you could ask me that I should deny . . . this is not a boon. . . . Nay, When I have a suit/Wherein I mean to touch your love indeed,/It shall be full of poise and difficult weight,/And fearful to be granted.*	She pleads powerfully Cassio's cause, arguing that Othello is doing himself a favor by taking Cassio back. She almost never thinks of the consequences for herself.
III,iii, 88–89	*Be as your fancies teach you. /Whate'er you be, I am obedient.*	She is quite capable of the strength that accompanies obedience to one's vows.
III,iii, 189	*For she had eyes, and chose me.*	Othello acknowledges the courage of his wife's action in choosing him. When he refers to her eyes, he is not unaware he is black.
V,ii, 124	*Nobody—I myself [have "done this deed"].*	Her final act is to shield her husband.
Generosity (Goodness)		
II,i, 254–255	*I cannot believe that in her. She's full of most blessed condition.*	Roderigo's reply to Iago's suggestion that Desdemona is unfaithful indicates that even this fool is aware of the influence for good which Desdemona exerts.
11,iii, 323–328	*She is of so free, so kind, so apt, so blessed a disposition she holds it a vice in her goodness not to do more than she is requested.*	Iago can tell the truth about a character, even to another, when it so suits his purpose.
II,iii, 366–368	*So will I turn her virtue into pitch,/And out of her own goodness make the net/That shall enmesh them all.*	And, of course, it is Desdemona's kindness in interceding for Cassio that is in part responsible for her death.
III,iii, 21–28	*. . . I'll perform it/To the last article. My lord shall never rest; . . . I'll intermingle everything he does/With Cassio's suit. . . . For thy solicitor shall rather die/Than give thy cause away.*	Another indication of her exceeding devotion to a cause— a devotion which even leads her into what might be called nagging.

Generosity (Goodness)	Quotation	Comment
III,iv, 122–124	*Alas . . . My advocation is not now in tune./My lord is not my lord; . . .*	His wrath saddens her, but she is unfaltering in her loyalty to Cassio and his cause.
III,iv, 130–131	*What I can do I will; and more I will/Than for myself I dare.*	Eagerness to do more than she is asked characterizes Desdemona, and Iago uses this against her.
III,iv, 150–154	*Beshrew me . . . I was (unhandsome warrior as I am!) /Arraigning his unkindness with my soul;/But now I find I had suborn'd the witness,/ And he's indicted falsely.*	The generosity which Iago describes (cf. II,iii,323–368) is illustrated here in her refusal to think ill of her husband.

Innocence

III,iii, 282–287	*Why do you speak so faintly? /Are you not well? . . . I have a pain upon my forehead, here. . . . Faith, that's with watching; 'twill away again./Let me but bind it hard, . . . It will be well.*	Another person's suspicions might have been aroused by Othello's manner. Desdemona is merely filled with solicitude.
III,iv, 23–29	*Where should I lose that handkerchief, . . . Believe me, I had rather have lost my purse . . .; and but my noble Moor/Is true of mind, and made of no such baseness/ As jealous creatures are, it were enough/To put him to ill thinking.*	To most critics these lines indicate that Desdemona is so pure and simple that no evil may be entertained in her mind. She does mention jealousy, but it becomes only too clear that she knows nothing about "ill thinking."
III,iv, 75–83	*I' faith? Is't true? . . . Then would to God I had never seen 't! . . . Why do you speak so startingly and rash? . . . It is not lost. But what an if it were?*	Othello frightens her with the story of the handkerchief, and she lies about it. Some critics condemn her for this; others take it as further indication of her delicacy and femininity.
III,iv, 140–150	*Something sure of state, . . . Hath puddled his clear spirit; and in such cases/Men's natures wrangle with inferior things, . . . Nay, we must think men are not gods,/Nor of them look for such observancy/As fits the bridal.*	Desdemona makes all possible allowances for her husband's wild conduct. Her mind refuses to acknowledge the evil of which he may be capable.
IV,iii, 61–63	*Dost thou in conscience think . . . That there be women do abuse their husbands/In such gross kind?*	She is lacking in worldly wisdom and cannot understand the baser passions—including jealousy.
V,ii, 76	*Alas, he is betray'd, and I undone!*	She lacks even the cunning to save herself. What she says throughout this scene shows

Innocence	*Quotation*	*Comment*
		her innocence of the nature of passion.
V,ii, 199–200	. . . *thou hast kill'd the sweetest innocent/That e'er did lift up eye.*	This is the final and definitive statement of Desdemona's innocence. It is made by Emilia, who knows her mistress well, even though to her innocence is an impractical virtue.

Gentleness
(Delicacy)

I,ii, 25	*But that I love the gentle Desdemona, . . .*	Othello is referring to a true gentleness, of both birth and manner, in Desdemona.
I,ii, 66–68	*. . . a maid so tender, fair, and happy,/So opposite to marriage that she shunn'd/The wealthy curled darlings of our nation, . . .*	Brabantio is blind to the fact that in rejecting the curled darlings for an older, stronger man she has lived up to his evaluation of her character.
I,iii, 94–96	*A maiden never bold;/Of spirit so still and quiet that her motion/Blush'd at herself; . . .*	Quite true, but her father has failed to notice the warrior-like qualities in his daughter.
I,iii, 98	*To fall in love with what she fear'd to look on!*	Desdemona, as her father says, is modest and shy. He underestimates, however, her strength of mind.

Beauty
(Graciousness)

II,i, 61–62	*He hath achiev'd a maid/That paragons description and wild fame; . . .*	Cassio joins in the chorus which sings her praises. All acknowledge her charm and goodness.
II,iii, 18–28	*. . . and she is sport for Jove. /She's a most exquisite lady. . . . a most fresh and delicate creature. . . . An inviting eye; and yet methinks right modest. . . . She is indeed perfection.*	Iago is characterizing Desdemona's outward appearance here. He cannot, however, trap Cassio into a derogatory remark about her character.
III,iii, 184–186	*To say my wife is fair, feeds well, loves company,/Is free of speech, sings, plays, and dances well./Where virtue is, these are more virtuous.*	Desdemona, for all her gentleness, is not predominantly shy or retiring. She is an accomplished Venetian lady, versed in all the graces that the Renaissance thought admirable in a woman of breeding.
IV,i, 188–207	*A fine woman! a fair woman! a sweet woman! . . . O, the world hath not a sweeter creature! . . . So delicate*	Othello cannot believe that a woman of such outward beauty and culture can be inwardly foul or vulgar. "The

Beauty (Graciousness)	Quotation	Comment
	with her needle! an admirable musician! O, she will sing the savageness out of a bear! Of so high and plenteous wit and invention! . . . And then, of so gentle a condition! . . . O Iago, the pity of it, Iago!	pity of it" would not be so poignant if Desdemona were not to all appearances ideal and the "necessary" sacrifice so costly and irreparable.
IV,iii, 4	*Your Honour is most welcome.*	In the midst of rather trying circumstances her charm does not desert her.

CASSIO

Physical Appearance		
I,iii, 398–404	*Cassio's a proper man. . . . He hath a person and a smooth dispose/To be suspected—fram'd to make women false.*	Cassio, as Iago acknowledges, is a handsome and genial young man—of a sort to tempt perhaps not too discerning women (like Bianca) rather than one of Desdemona's temper.
Intemperance (Rashness, Drunkenness)		
II,i, 279	*. . . he is rash and very sudden in choler, . . .*	He is easily angered or upset, as the drinking scene indicates.
II,iii, 34–44	*I have very poor and unhappy brains for drinking. . . . I am unfortunate in the infirmity and dare not task my weakness with any more.*	Cassio realizes this weakness and resists it. Like Othello, he might never have succumbed to his temptation had it not been for Iago.
II,iii, 49	*I'll do't, but it dislikes me.*	His conviviality, abetted by Iago, gets the better of him, and he agrees to have a few more drinks.
Character (Reputation)		
II,iii, 262–265	*Reputation, reputation, reputation! . . . I have lost the immortal part of myself, and what remains is bestial.*	One of several statements in the play of the reputation theme. The loss of reputation means more to Cassio than anything else, and he is perhaps over-anxious in his efforts to get back into Othello's favor.

Character (Reputation)	Quotation	Comment
II,iii, 278–280	*I will rather sue to be despis'd than to deceive so good a commander with so slight, so drunken, and so indiscreet an officer.*	There is something almost hysterical in Cassio's sense of shame. Like Othello, he is a very proud man, but he is more childish than Othello in his maudlin reaction to humiliation.
III,iii, 70–73	*Michael Cassio,/That came a-wooing with you, and . . . When I have spoke of you dispraisingly,/Hath ta'en your part— . . .*	He quite good-naturedly stood up for Othello during the latter's courtship. His character is open and generous.
Soldiership I,i, 19–24	*. . . a great arithmetician, . . . That never set a squadron in the field,/Nor the division of a battle knows/More than a spinster; . . .*	Cassio has evidently been trained in military tactics from books rather than from experience. In the Renaissance a bitter controversy raged between the combat type of soldier (Iago) and the bookish theoretician (Cassio).
I,i, 26–27	*Mere prattle, without practice,/Is all his soldiership. But he, sir, had th' election; . . .*	Cassio is probably of nobler birth than Iago and perhaps has letters from influential persons. Modern critics continue the debate as to whether Othello acted wisely in making Cassio his lieutenant.

EMILIA

Loyalty III,iii, 3–4	*I warrant it grieves my husband/As if the cause were his.*	Emilia is as much deceived by her husband as are the other characters. But she is loyal, ultimately, only to righteousness.
III,iii, 290–299	*I am glad I have found this napkin. . . . My wayward husband hath a hundred times/Woo'd me to steal it; . . . What he will do with it heaven knows, not I;/I nothing but to please his fantasy.*	A difficult remark in terms of Emilia's later expression of dismay when she finds out what her husband has done with the handkerchief. The present speech indicates, however, that she loves Iago and so far has little cause to distrust him. Nevertheless, her divided ideals and loyalties in the play as a whole present a problem.

Loyalty	*Quotation*	*Comment*
III,iii, 314–318	*What will you do with't, that you have been so earnest/To have me filch it? . . . If it be not for some purpose of import,/Give't me again. Poor lady, she'll run mad/When she shall lack it.*	Though curious about his purposes, she does not rebuke her husband's rudeness.
IV,ii, 12–18	*I durst, my lord, to wager she is honest, . . . For if she be not honest, . . . There's no man happy; . . .*	She is capable of the same loyalty to her mistress as to her husband, as she proves later.
IV,ii, 136–147	*A halter pardon him! and hell gnaw his bones! . . . Some such squire he was/That turn'd your wit the seamy side without/And made you to suspect me with the Moor.*	She is outspoken in reviling anyone who slurs the reputation of Desdemona. Also, there is no reason to believe that Iago sees any convincing cause to suspect his wife of disloyalty. (But cf. I,iii, 392–394.)
V,ii, 155–157	*If he say so, may his pernicious soul/Rot half a grain a day! he lies to th' heart./She was too fond of her most filthy bargain.*	After her initial shock, anger at her husband's lies seizes her, and she demonstrates her loyalty to Desdemona.
V,ii, 218–226	*O God! O heavenly pow'rs! . . . O thou dull Moor, that handkerchief thou speak'st of/I found by fortune, and did give my husband; . . .*	She will speak the truth, come what might. It is this that leads one to believe she is speaking the truth when she tells Desdemona she knows nothing about the handkerchief. Within the limits of a rather generous moral code, she is a virtuous woman, loyal to what she judges to be right.
Shrewdness (Worldliness)		
III,iv, 99	*Is not this man jealous?*	The shrewdness and worldly wisdom which enable her to interpret this sort of emotion have not helped her to understand her own husband.
III,iv, 103–106	*'Tis not a year or two shows us a man. . . . They eat us hungerly, and when they are full,/They belch us.*	She has learned much (including a robust vocabulary) from having a husband like Iago.
III,iv, 160–161	*They are not jealous for the cause,/But jealous for they are jealous.*	Emilia points out the irrational workings of emotion to Desdemona, who tries to find a reasonable cause for Othello's behavior.

Shrewdness (Worldliness)	Quotation	Comment
IV,iii, 69–77	*The world's a huge thing. It is a great price for a small vice. . . . I would not do such a thing for a joint-ring, . . . but, for all the whole world—*	In place of Desdemona's uncompromising purity, Emilia has a rather humorously worldly approach to sex.
IV,iii, 89–106	*But I do think it is their husbands' faults/If wives do fall. . . . have we not affections, . . . let them know,/ The ills we do, their ills instruct us so.*	She has observed enough of life to make some telling comments upon the ways of men. Yet she, in her tolerant shrewdness, is no female counterpart of her husband.
Thoughtlessness		
III,iv, 23–24	*Where should I lose that handkerchief, Emilia?/I know not, madam.*	Critics debate whether Emilia is silly, protecting her husband, or simply thoughtless in this speech.
V,ii, 149–152	*My husband? . . . My husband say that she was false?*	She is genuinely startled that it is Iago who is the villain, though the handkerchief episode should have caused suspicion. Often shrewd people miss what is under their noses.
Commonness		
II,i, 101–103	*. . . would she give you so much of her lips/As of her tongue she oft bestows on me, /You would have enough.*	Iago is not to be trusted in his remarks about other people. Emilia is a rather common wife, but not deserving of the abuse he jovially heaps upon her.
III,iii, 302–304	*It is a common thing— . . . To have a foolish wife.*	Iago is the sort of man given to this gross teasing—it is part of what characterizes him as a "good fellow," and seems to please Emilia.
IV,ii, 20	*. . . yet she's a simple bawd . . .*	Othello underestimates Emilia's native shrewdness and sense of right—but so does her husband.

RODERIGO

Stupidity (Gullibility)		
I,iii, 389	*Thus do I ever make my fool my purse.*	Roderigo is Iago's easiest victim, serving as a source of

Stupidity (Gullibility)	Quotation	Comment
		revenue and also an agent for his schemes. Roderigo was an Elizabethan gull—what we would today call a sucker.
II,iii, 373–387	*. . . I shall have so much experience for my pains; and so, with no money at all, and a little more wit, return again to Venice. . . . Away, I say! Thou shalt know more hereafter.*	It dawns on Roderigo that things are not going particularly well—that he is no nearer than before to seducing Desdemona. But Iago reassures him.
IV,ii, 174–185	*I do not find that thou deal'st justly with me. . . . your words and performance are no kin together.*	This is an understatement, but by deft, though not subtle, flattery, Iago puts off the reckoning.
IV,ii, 191–193	*You have told me she hath receiv'd them, and return'd me expectations and comforts of sudden respect and acquaintance, but I find none.*	It never occurs to him that Iago has kept the jewels. He merely blames Desdemona for not responding.
V,i, 11–12	*I have rubb'd this young quat almost to the sense,/And he grows angry.*	Iago realizes he has pushed Roderigo too far. Like Emilia, this fool will be an unsuspected agent of Iago's undoing.

6. Critical Commentaries

The following critical selections represent some of the best and also some of the most controversial criticism of *Othello* dating from the century when the play was written until the present day. Readers will notice the way in which critics reflect their own era (as does Thomas Rymer), their geographical region (as does Mary Preston), and their own critical approach (as does F. R. Leavis). Shakespearean critics also tend to write more about subjects that present a problem of interpretation. Thus there has probably been more criticism of Iago than of Othello himself.

Othello has engaged the minds of some of our finest men of letters. In the following pages the student will find writers famous in their own right, including Samuel Johnson, Samuel Taylor Coleridge, William Hazlitt, and T. S. Eliot. So full of insights has *Othello* criticism been—insights that frequently go beyond the play to speculations about the ways of God and man—that this body of criticism constitutes, almost independently, an important commentary upon life.

For the reader's convenience in following the current and patterns of *Othello* criticism through the centuries, this criticism has been chronologically arranged, and the date of publication has been placed at the head of each selection.

THOMAS RYMER [1] [1693]

What ever rubs or difficulty may stick on the Bark, the Moral, sure, of this Fable is very instructive.

1. First, This may be a caution to all Maidens of Quality how, without their Parents consent, they run away with Blackamoors.

. . . .

Secondly, This may be a warning to all good Wives, that they look well to their Linnen.

Thirdly, This may be a lesson to Husbands, that before their Jealousie be Tragical, the proofs may be Mathematical.

. . . .

In the *Neighing* of an Horse, or in the *growling* of a Mastiff, there is a meaning, there is an lively expression, and may I say, more humanity, than many times in the Tragical flights of *Shakespear*.

Step then amongst the Scenes to observe the Conduct in this Tragedy.

The first we see are *Jago* and *Roderigo*, by Night in the Streets of *Venice*. After growling a long time together, they resolve to tell *Brabantio* that his Daughter is run away with the Black-a-moor. *Jago* and *Roderigo* were not of quality to be familiar with *Brabantio*, nor had any provocation from him, to deserve a rude thing at their hands. *Brabantio* was a Noble Venetian, one of the Sovereign Lords and principal persons in the Government, Peer to the most Serene *Doge*, one attended with more state, ceremony and punctillio, than any English Duke, or Nobleman in the Government will pretend to. This misfortune in his Daughter is so prodigious, so tender a point, as might puzzle the finest Wit of the most *supersubtle* Venetian to touch upon it, or break the discovery to her Father. See then how delicately *Shakespear* minces the matter:

[1] *A Short View of Tradegy*, in *The Critical Works of Thomas Rymer*, ed. Curt A. Zimansky (New Haven: Yale University Press, 1956), pp. 132, 136, 138, 160, 164.

Rod. *What ho*, Brabantio, *Signior* Brabantio, *ho*.
Jago. *Awake, what ho*, Brabantio,
Thieves, thieves, thieves:
Look to your House, your Daughter, and your Bags
Thieves, thieves.

. . . .

But besides the Manners to a *Magnifico*, humanity cannot bear that an old Gentleman in his misfortune should be insulted over with such a rabble of Skoundrel language, when no cause or provocation. Yet thus it is on our Stage, this is our School of good manners, and the *Speculum Vitæ*.

But our *Magnifico* is here in the dark, nor are yet his Robes on: attend him to the Senate house, and there see the difference, see the effects of Purple.

. . . .

So much ado, so much stress, so much passion and repetition about an Handkerchief! Why was not this call'd the *Tragedy of the Handkerchief*? . . . Had it been *Desdemona's* Garter, the Sagacious Moor might have smelt a Rat: but the Handkerchief is so remote a trifle, no Booby, on this side *Mauritania*, cou'd make any consequence from it.

. . . .

There is in this Play, some burlesk, some humour, and ramble of Comical Wit, some shew, and some Mimickry to divert the spectators: but the tragical part is, plainly none other, than a Bloody Farce, without salt or savour.

SAMUEL JOHNSON [1] [1765]

The beauties of this play impress themselves so strongly upon the attention of the reader, that they can draw no aid from critical illustration. The fiery openness of *Othello*, magnanimous, artless, and credulous, boundless in his confidence, ardent in his affection, inflexible in his resolution, and obdurate in his revenge; the cool malignity of *Iago*, silent in his resentment, subtle in his designs, and studious at once of his interest and his vengeance; the soft simplicity of *Desdemona*, confident of merit, and conscious of innocence, her artless perseverance in her suit, and her slowness to

[1] *Johnson on Shakespeare,* ed. Walter Raleigh (London: Oxford University Press, 1908; reprinted, 1949), pp. 200–201.

suspect that she can be suspected, are such proofs of *Shakespeare's* skill in human nature, as, I suppose, it is vain to seek in any modern writer. The gradual progress which Iago makes in the Moor's conviction, and the circumstances which he employs to inflame him, are so artfully natural, that, though it will perhaps not be said of him as he says of himself, that he is *a man not easily jealous,* yet we cannot but pity him when at last we find him *perplexed in the extreme.*

. . . .

The Scenes from the beginning to the end are busy, varied by happy interchanges, and regularly promoting the progression of the story; and the narrative in the end, though it tells but what is known already, yet is necessary to produce the death of *Othello.*

Had the scene opened in *Cyprus,* and the preceding incidents been occasionally related, there had been little wanting to a drama of the most exact and scrupulous regularity.

SAMUEL TAYLOR COLERIDGE [1]

[1849; written as early as 1802]

Iago's speech:—

Virtue? a fig! 'tis in ourselves, that we are thus, or thus, etc.

This speech comprises the passionless character of Iago. It is all will in intellect; and therefore he is here a bold partizan of a truth, but yet of a truth converted into a falsehood by the absence of all the necessary modifications caused by the frail nature of man. And then comes the last sentiment,—

Our raging motions, our carnal stings, our unbitted lusts, whereof I take this, that you call—love, to be a sect or scion!

Here is the true Iagoism of, alas! how many! Note Iago's pride of mastery in the repetition of "Go, make money!" to his anticipated dupe, even stronger than his love of lucre: and when Roderigo is completely won—

I am chang'd. I'll go sell all my land—

when the effect has been fully produced, the repetition of triumph—

Go to; farewell; put money enough in your purse!

[1] *Notes and Lectures upon Shakespeare and Some of the Old Poets and Dramatists* (London: William Pickering, 1849), Vol. I, pp. 261–262.

The remainder—Iago's soliloquy—the motive-hunting of a motiveless malignity—how awful it is! Yea, whilst he is still allowed to bear the divine image, it is too fiendish for his own steady view,—for the lonely gaze of a being next to devil, and only not quite devil,—and yet a character which Shakespeare has attempted and executed, without disgust and without scandal!

WILLIAM HAZLITT [1] [1817]

The character of Iago is one of the supererogations of Shakespeare's genius. Some persons, more nice than wise, have thought this whole character unnatural, because his villainy is *without a sufficient motive*. Shakespeare, who was as good a philosopher as he was a poet, thought otherwise. He knew that the love of power, which is another name for the love of mischief, is natural to man. He would know this as well or better than if it had been demonstrated to him by a logical diagram, merely from seeing children paddle in the dirt or kill flies for sport. Iago in fact belongs to a class of character, common to Shakespeare and at the same time peculiar to him; whose heads are as acute and active as their hearts are hard and callous. Iago is to be sure an extreme instance of the kind; that is to say, of diseased intellectual activity, with the most perfect indifference to moral good or evil, or rather with a decided preference of the latter, because it falls more readily in with his favourite propensity, gives greater zest to his thoughts and scope to his actions. He is quite or nearly as indifferent to his own fate as to that of others; he runs all risks for a trifling and doubtful advantage; and is himself the dupe and victim of his ruling passion—an insatiable craving after action of the most difficult and dangerous kind. "Our ancient" is a philosopher, who fancies that a lie that kills has more point in it than an alliteration or an antithesis; who thinks a fatal experiment on the peace of a family a better thing than watching the palpitations in the heart of a flea in a microscope; who plots the ruin of his friends as an exercise for his ingenuity, and stabs men in the dark to prevent ennui. His gaiety, such as it is, arises from the success of his treachery; his ease from the torture he has inflicted on others. He is an amateur of tragedy in real life, and instead of employing his invention on imaginary characters, or long-forgotten incidents, he takes the bolder and more desperate course of getting up his plot at home, casts the principal parts among his nearest friends and connections, and rehearses it in downright earnest, with steady nerves and unabated resolution.

[1] *The Round Table and Characters of Shakespeare's Plays* (New York: E. P. Dutton, 1944), pp. 206–207.

MARY PRESTON [1] [1869]

In studying the play of *Othello*, I have always *imagined* its hero a *white* man. It is true the dramatist paints him black, but this shade does not suit the man. It is a stage decoration, which *my taste* discards; a fault of color from an artistic point of view. I have, therefore, as I have before stated in *my readings* of this play, dispensed with it. Shakespeare was too correct a delineator of human nature to have colored Othello *black*, if he had personally acquainted himself with the idiosyncrasies of the African race.

We may regard, then, the daub of black upon Othello's portrait as an *ebullition* of fancy, a *freak* of imagination,—the visionary conception of an ideal figure,—one of the few erroneous strokes of the great master's brush, the *single* blemish on a faultless work.

Othello *was* a *white* man.

ALGERNON SWINBURNE [2] [1880]

. . . [Coleridge] has left on everlasting record the deliberate expression of his judgment that *Othello* combines and unites the qualities of *King Lear*, "the most tremendous effort of Shakespeare as a poet" (a verdict with which I may venture to express my full and absolute agreement), and of *Hamlet*, his most tremendous effort "as a philosopher or meditator." It may be so: and Coleridge may be right in his estimate that "*Othello* is the union of the two." I should say myself, but with no thought of setting my opinion against that of the man who at his best was now and then the greatest of all poets and all critics, that the fusion of thought and passion, inspiration and meditation, was at its height in *King Lear*. But in *Othello* we get the pure poetry of natural and personal emotion, unqualified by the righteous doubt and conscientious intelligence which instigate and impede the will and the action of Hamlet. The collision and the contrast of passion and intellect, of noble passion and infernal intellect, was never before and can never be again presented and verified as in this most tragic of all tragedies that ever the supreme student of humanity bequeathed for the study of all time. As a poet and a thinker Æschylus was the equal, if not the superior, of Shakespeare; as a creator, a revealer, and an interpreter, infinite in his insight and his truthfulness, his tenderness and his wisdom, his

[1] *Studies in Shakespeare* (Philadelphia: Claxton, Remsen & Haffelfinger, 1869), p. 71.

[2] *Prose Works*, in *The Complete Works of Algernon Charles Swinburne*, ed. Sir Edmund Gosse and Thomas James Wise (London: William Heineman Ltd., 1926), XI, 253–254.

justice and his mercy, no man who ever lived can stand beside the author of *Othello*.

A. C. BRADLEY [1] [1904]

Of all Shakespeare's tragedies, . . . not even excepting *King Lear*, *Othello* is the most painfully exciting and the most terrible. From the moment when the temptation of the hero begins, the reader's heart and mind are held in a vice, experiencing the extremes of pity and fear, sympathy and repulsion, sickening hope and dreadful expectation.

. . . .

Let me first set aside a mistaken view. I do not mean the ridiculous notion that Othello was jealous by temperament, but the idea, which has some little plausibility, that the play is primarily a study of a noble barbarian, who has become a Christian and has imbibed some of the civilisation of his employers, but who retains beneath the surface the savage passions of his Moorish blood and also the suspiciousness regarding female chastity common among Oriental peoples, and that the last three Acts depict the outburst of these original feelings through the thin crust of Venetian culture. . . . I do not mean that Othello's race is a matter of no account. . . . But in regard to the essentials of his character it is not important. . . .

. . . .

This character is so noble, . . . and his sufferings are so heart-rending, that he stirs . . . in most readers a passion of mingled love and pity which they feel for no other hero in Shakespeare. . . . Yet there are some critics . . . who cherish a grudge against him. They do not merely think that in the later stages of his temptation he showed a certain obtuseness, and that, to speak pedantically, he acted with unjustifiable precipitance and violence; no one, I suppose, denies that. But, even when they admit that he was not of a jealous temper, they consider that he *was* "easily jealous"; they seem to think that it was inexcusable in him to feel any suspicion of his wife at all; and they blame him for never suspecting Iago or asking him for evidence. . . .

Othello . . . was trustful, and thorough in his trust. He put entire confidence in the honesty of Iago, who had not only been his companion in arms, but, as he believed, had just proved his faithfulness in the matter of the marriage. This confidence was misplaced, and we happen to know it; but it was no sign of stupidity in Othello.

[1] *Shakespearean Tragedy* (London: The Macmillan Company, 1904; reprinted by World Publishing Company, Meridian Books, 1955), pp. 145–158.

For his opinion of Iago was the opinion of practically everyone who knew him: and that opinion was that Iago was before all things "honest,". . .

Iago does not bring these warnings to a husband who had lived with a wife for months and years and knew her like his sister or his bosom-friend. . . . But he was newly married; in the circumstances he cannot have known much of Desdemona before his marriage; . . .

. . . In Othello's case, after a long and most artful preparation, there now come . . . the suggestions that he is not an Italian, nor even a European; that he is totally ignorant of the thoughts and the customary morality of Venetian women; that he had himself seen in Desdemona's deception of her father how perfect an actress she could be. As he listens in horror, for a moment at least the past is revealed to him in a new and dreadful light, and the ground seems to sink under his feet. These suggestions are followed by a tentative but hideous and humiliating insinuation of what his honest and much-experienced friend fears may be the true explanation of Desdemona's rejection of acceptable suitors, and of her strange, and naturally temporary, preference for a black man. . . .

Now I repeat that *any* man situated as Othello was would have been disturbed by Iago's communications, and I add that many men would have been made wildly jealous.

T. S. ELIOT [1] [1927]

. . . What Othello seems to me to be doing in making this speech ["Soft you; a word or two before you go."] is *cheering himself up*. He is endeavouring to escape reality, he has ceased to think about Desdemona, and is thinking about himself. Humility is the most difficult of all virtues to achieve; nothing dies harder than the desire to think well of oneself. Othello succeeds in turning himself into a pathetic figure, by adopting an *aesthetic* rather than a moral attitude, dramatising himself against his environment. He takes in the spectator, but the human motive is primarily to take in himself. I do not believe that any writer has ever exposed this *bovarysme,* the human will to see things as they are not, more clearly than Shakespeare.

G. WILSON KNIGHT [2] [1930]

. . . As all within *Othello*—save the Iago-theme—is separated, differentiated, solidified, so the play itself seems at first to be divorced

[1] "Shakespeare and the Stoicism of Seneca," *Selected Essays of T. S. Eliot,* 3d rev. ed. (London: Faber and Faber Ltd., 1951), pp. 130–131.
[2] *The Wheel of Fire* (Oxford University Press, 1930; Barnes & Noble, Inc., 1964; reprinted by World Publishing Company, Meridian Books, 1963), pp. 118–119.

from wider issues, a lone thing of meaningless beauty in the Shakespearian universe, solitary, separate, unyielding and chaste as the moon. It is unapproachable, yields itself to no easy mating with our minds. Its thought does not readily mesh with our thought. We can visualize it, admire its concrete felicities of phrase and image, the mosaic of its language, the sculptural outline of its effects, the precision and chastity of its form. But one cannot be lost in it, subdued to it, enveloped by it, as one is drenched and refreshed by the elemental cataracts of *King Lear;* one cannot be intoxicated by it as by the rich wine of *Antony and Cleopatra*. *Othello* is essentially outside us, beautiful with a lustrous, planetary beauty. Yet the Iago-conception is of a different kind from the rest of the play. This conception alone, if no other reason existed, would point the necessity of an intellectual interpretation. So we see the Iago-spirit gnawing at the root of all the *Othello* values, the *Othello* beauties; he eats into the core and heart of this romantic world, worms his way into its solidity, rotting it, poisoning it. Once this is clear, the whole play begins to have meaning. On the plane of dramatic humanity, we see a story of the cynic intriguing to ruin the soldier and his love. On the plane of poetic conception, in matters of technique, style, personification— there we see a spirit of negation, colourless, and undefined, attempting to make chaos of a world of stately, architectural, and exquisitely coloured forms. . . . Thus the different technique of the Othello and Iago conceptions is intrinsic with the plot of the play: in them we have the spirit of negation set against the spirit of creation. That is why Iago is undefined, devisualized, inhuman, in a play of consummate skill in concrete imagery and vivid delineation. He is a colourless and ugly thing in a world of colour and harmony. His failure lies in this: in the final scene, at the moment of his complete triumph, Emilia dies for her mistress to the words of Desdemona's willow-song, and the *Othello* music itself sounds with a nobler cadence, a richer flood of harmonies, a more selfless and universalized flight of the imagination than before. The beauties of the *Othello* world are not finally disintegrated: they make "a swan-like end, fading in music."

ELMER EDGAR STOLL [1] [1933]

Mr. T. S. Eliot takes this final phase of the hero psychologically— he is "cheering himself up. He is endeavouring to escape reality, . . . turning himself into a pathetic figure, by adopting an *aesthetic* rather than a moral attitude, dramatising himself against his environment." Something the same the critic finds in Hamlet, Antony, and Coriolanus, as they face the end. Are these, then, now only playing a

[1] *Art and Artifice in Shakespeare* (New York: Cambridge University Press, 1933; reprinted by Barnes and Noble, Inc., 1962), pp. 173–174.

part, like a Thackeray fribble or coquette? As I have shown elsewhere this is a self-descriptive method, as in Chapman and Marston, and in Seneca before them, and not merely at the end of a play, nor merely in connection with the hero: if taken as a bit of self-consciousness, it much troubles the noble and heroic impression. But the main matter in question is one of rhythm; Othello, obscured, must shine forth again; maddened, he must come to his senses; stained with a hideous crime, he must see and show himself as he is. And even as dramatic psychology—that is, such as does not press and peer behind drama and poetry—the speech is finely appropriate. After such an experience and such depths of despair Othello must, in sheer reaction and relapse, think a little well of himself. It is one of the glories of Shakespeare that, unlike the French classicists, he recognizes the limits of human nature: it is also one of the sources of his dramatic effect. Both the one truth and the other are exemplified also at the end of Lear.

CAROLINE F. E. SPURGEON [1] [1935]

The evil smell of sin is in *Othello* as constantly kept before us as are its foulness and dirt. When Iago tentatively suggests to Othello that in choosing to marry him—a black man—Desdemona has already shown a perverted and unnatural taste, he exclaims:

> Foh! one may smell in such a will most rank,
> Foul disproportion, thoughts unnatural.

. . . and Othello brings out the horror of the contrast between the fair looks of Desdemona and what he believes her deeds entirely by means of smell, lamenting,

> O thou weed
> Who art so lovely fair and smell'st so sweet
> That the sense aches at thee, would thou hadst
> ne'er been born!

and answering her piteous query,

> Alas, what ignorant sin have I committed?

with the agonised cry,

> What committed!
> Heaven stops the nose at it.

. . . .

[1] *Shakespeare's Imagery* (New York: The Macmillan Company; Cambridge, England: At the University Press, 1935, reprinted by Beacon Press, 1958), pp. 161–162, 335–336.

In *Othello* we see a low type of life, insects and reptiles, swarming
and preying on each other, not out of special ferocity, but just in
accordance with their natural instincts, mischievous and irresponsible
wild cats, goats and monkeys, or the harmless, innocent animal
trapped or beaten. This reflects and repeats the spectacle of the
wanton torture of one human being by another, which we witness
in the tragedy, the human spider and his fly. . . .

LEO KIRSCHBAUM [1] [1944]

In short, it seems to me that by means of Iago's soliloquies; by
means of character contrast with the brutally clear-eyed Iago, the
earthy Emilia, the self-honest Cassio (who, also, be it remembered,
openly admits his relationship to Bianca); by means of action contrast in the rejoinders of Roderigo, Cassio and Emilia to the proposal
that Desdemona is unchaste; by means of Othello's own words in
the first and second acts; by means of a carefully drawn Othello
in the temptation scene who considers himself much stronger than
he actually is; by means of sundry touches throughout which show
Othello refusing to recognize his own passionate nature; by means
of a broken Othello in the last act, who tries to hang on to his nobility
by refusing to face the fact of his murder—by means of all this
Shakespeare has shown us that his hero is not as strong or as good a
man as he thinks he is, that the hero's flaw is his refusal to face the
reality of his own nature. This Othello, who (I think) is the Othello
Shakespeare intended to convey, is rather different from the modern
Othello, who is always thoroughly noble—before, during, and after
his downfall. . . .

The Othello that Shakespeare presents is nobly tragic in the same
sense in which Macbeth and Antony and Coriolanus and Lear are
nobly tragic. Shakespeare's tragic protagonist is noble, but he is not
altogether noble. He represents Aristotle's dictum:

> A man not preeminently virtuous and just, whose misfortune, how-
> ever, is brought upon him not by vice or depravity but by some
> error of judgment, he being one of those who enjoy great reputa-
> tion and prosperity. . . . The change in the hero's fortunes must
> be . . . from happiness to misery; and the cause of it must lie
> not in any depravity, but in some great error on his part; the
> man himself being either such as we have described, or better,
> not worse, than that. (*Poetics*, Chapter 13)

[1] "The Modern Othello," *ELH, A Journal of English Literary History*, XI
(1944), pp. 283–296, quote 295–296.

It is not the hero's nobility in Shakespeare's tragedies but the flaw, the sin or error that all flesh is heir to, that destroys him. It is the close interweaving of great man, mere man, and base man that makes of Othello the peculiarly powerful and mysterious figure he is. In him Shakespeare shows the possible greatness, the possible baseness not only closely allied in what is after all mere man but also so causally connected that one must perforce wonder and weep.

HARLEY GRANVILLE-BARKER [1] [1945]

We could take it . . . that this opening view of Iago, the first impression he is to make, was meant to be the true one, if only because Shakespeare, in first presenting a character, never deliberately misleads us, is accustomed, rather, to sketch in its chief features, then and there, as unmistakably as possible, so as to leave us in no doubt from the start as to the sort of man or woman this is. . . . And here, in the first two scenes, in the contrast between the men, and in the boasted hate and its masking, are the main factors of the play already defined and set in motion. . . . With Macbeth, with Antony, amid the clashes of *King Lear,* the destructive force is one of the nobler human ardours turned to evil, and the battle-ground—as so notably with Hamlet—is the hero's soul. Here the evil impulse is externalized in Iago; and if Othello's soul be a battle-ground, he himself puts up no fight on it. Nor can the jealousy which undoes him be properly called a degrading of the love it supplants; it is an aberration rather, a craze, and an ignoble one. Iago inoculates him with it, as with a disease, and after the feeblest of struggles—he is lost. *Othello* is not, therefore, a spiritual tragedy in the sense that the others may be called so. It is only the more painful for that; an all but intolerable exhibition, indeed, of human wickedness and folly, which does not so much purge us with pity and terror as fill us with horror and with anger that such a shoddy creature as Iago, possessed by his mountebank egoism, his envy and spite, should be able unresisted to destroy an Othello and bring Desdemona to her death. This incongruity is the keynote of the tragedy, and Shakespeare, therefore, strikes it clearly to begin with. And the actor who tries, here or later, to present Iago as a sort of half-brother to Milton's Satan falsifies both character and play.

. . . .

[Iago] is a passionless creature. Cinthio gives his wicked Ensign some motive for evil doing in jealousy, and a love for Desdemona

[1] *Prefaces to Shakespeare,* 4th Series: *Othello* (London: Sidgwick and Jackson Ltd., 1945), pp. 155–156, 167–168.

ignored and so "changed into the bitterest hate." But Shakespeare admits neither love nor lust into Iago's composition, nothing so human; shows him to us, on the contrary, frigidly speculating upon the use such indulgence might be to him, and as frigidly deciding: none. Even his hate is cold, and will be the more tenacious for that, its strength not being spent in emotional ebb and flow. His endeavours then to respond suitably to Othello's outbursts—the flamboyant "Take note, take note, O world . . ." and the kneeling to echo and mock the oath by "yond marble heaven"—are simply histrionic, and overdone at that. And this, made plain to us, might be plain to Othello, were he not "eaten up with passion." For of intellectual excitement Iago *is* capable, and, elated by swift success, he begins to run risks. That stirs his cold blood; it is all that does.

ALFRED HARBAGE [1] [1947]

. . . The role of Desdemona is one of the most remarkable in Shakespeare. No woman in the plays is more pure than she, none whose every word is so compounded of kindliness, purity, and faith; and yet the aura of suspicion surrounding her is not purely of Iago's creation. Desdemona has married a Moor. About Othello's physical qualities we are left in no doubt. He is called "thick-lips" and "an old black ram." Elsewhere in Shakespeare, a black skin is viewed as revolting or as a symbol of evil. . . . Shakespeare retained the black skin of Cinthio's character and added a further disabling feature—middle-age. In his own words, Othello is declined "into a vale of years." In the popular mind of Shakespeare's time as of today the attraction of an Othello for a Desdemona would have only one explanation—the waywardness of lust; Hamlet's most virulent attack upon his mother is informed with suspicion and disgust provoked by the ugliness of Claudius. Another suspicion attaching to Desdemona at the outset arises from the deception she has practiced upon her father. All Shakespeare's maidens in love deceive their fathers (except Ophelia), but only Desdemona's is permitted to speak as Brabantio speaks,

> Look to her, Moor, if thou hast eyes to see.
> She has deceiv'd her father, and may thee.

We may say that the speech serves to sow a seed in Othello's mind, but it also sows one in ours. Cinthio tells us directly that in marrying a Moor the lady was "not drawn by female appetite." Shakespeare makes no such apology. Instead Iago is permitted to harp upon the theme with terrible vividness:

---

[1] *As They Liked It* (New York: The Macmillan Company, 1947; reprinted by Harper & Row, Torchbooks), pp. 64–66.

Foh! one may smell in such a will most rank,
Foul disproportion, thoughts unnatural—

Shakespeare counters both Iago's charges and our predisposition in the matter by changing the Moor from the stealthy assassin he is in Cinthio to a man a pure woman might love, and by elevating Desdemona to the point of idealization.

H. B. CHARLTON [1] [1948]

. . . Othello is incontestably black, black with the blackness of a Negro, not merely tinted with the sun-tan of the Hollywood sheik. "Black as mine own face," he says himself; "for that I am black," he repeats; and Brabantio refers in disgust to his "sooty bosom." Neither Coleridge nor Lamb could bring themselves to accept a negroid Othello. Coleridge would grant him a sort of indeterminate blackness, but nothing more negroid. Lamb would not even retain the colour, dissolving its momentary pictorial appearance into the poetic hues of Othello's moral brightness. But Othello is in fact negroid—"thick-lips" he is called. Another of Shakespeare's Moors, Aaron, in *Titus Andronicus*, is called by the Roman Titus "a coal-black Moor"; and Aaron himself described a fellow-Moor as a "thick-lipp'd slave."

. . . .

. . . [Othello] has through life relied hardly at all on the tutelage of intellect. Indeed, whereas his instinct and his nature strengthen themselves in the conflicts of a moral situation, an intellectual dilemma confounds his mind. He has neither faculty nor skill to resolve it. His reason is inadequate for dialectic, and his power of thought is not sufficiently acute to sift the likelihoods of problematic circumstance. He is inexpert in simple intellectual judgment; and the intellectual confusion which such effort induces in him gives further opportunity for his passion to break through its disciplined courses and submerge his whole apprehension. His mind is unequal to his soul. Hence his inevitable predicament:

No! to be once in doubt
Is once to be resolved.

But resolutions taken in such manner are neither guided by reason nor directed by moral nobility; they are determined and propelled by the sheer might of passion. Iago knows this and builds his evil

[1] *Shakespearian Tragedy* (Cambridge, England: At the University Press, 1948; reprinted in paperback), pp. 118–119, 123.

schemes on it: he knows Othello's nature, and with consummately audacious artistry, dares to rely on a plot so simple that Othello alone of all mankind is the one man certain to be caught by it.

WOLFGANG CLEMEN [1] [1951; original German edition, 1936]

The difference between Othello's and Iago's imagery—like everything else in Shakespeare—cannot be reduced to a simple formula. But of all the contradistinctions which might at least give us a hint of this difference, that existing between the concept of the static and of the dynamic comes closest to the real heart of the matter. Iago's images are static, because they are incapable of further inner growth, because the objects appear in a dry and lifeless manner, because . . . a narrow pattern of stylistic construction hinders the further development of the image. The prosaic brevity of Iago's images stands in contrast with the swelling opulence and poetic force of Othello's imagery. . . . Iago would be wholly incapable of the moving poetic language uttered by Othello; and, likewise, Othello could never be the author of Iago's cold and cynical utterances. In Othello's imagery everything is in movement, because everything springs from his own emotion. His images always appear at crucial points of his inner experience; the forcefulness and agitation of his images is an expression of his own passionate nature. Iago, on the other hand, stands not in an emotional, but in a rational relationship to his images.

. . . .

A closer examination of the content of Othello's and Iago's imagery reveals further characteristic differences. The objects named by Iago belong to a lower and purely material world, whereas the things alive in Othello's imagination generally belong to a higher sphere. Iago's imagery teems with repulsive animals of a low order; with references to eating and drinking and bodily functions and with technical and commercial terms. In Othello's language, however, the elements prevail—the heavens, the celestial bodies, the wind and the sea— the forces of nature, everything light and moving that corresponds best to his nature. At moments of intense emotion his imagery links heaven and hell together, bearing out his inner relation to the cosmic powers, and revealing the enormous dimensions and power of his imaginative conceptions. Hyperbole is therefore more often found in Othello's imagery than in that used by other Shakespearian heroes.

[1] *The Development of Shakespeare's Imagery* (Cambridge, Mass.: Harvard University Press, 1951; reprinted by Hill and Wang), pp. 123–125.

HAROLD C. GODDARD [1] [1951]

. . . Under the title of *A Practical Joke,* Dostoevsky's wife relates a domestic incident which occurred in the spring of 1876. . . .
. . . A new novel by Mme. Sophie Smirnov entitled *The Strong Character* was running as a serial. . . . In it . . . was published an anonymous letter . . . :

"Dear Sir, Noblest Peter Ivanovich,
    As I am a perfect stranger to you, but take an interest in your feelings, I venture to address these lines to you. . . . a certain person, who is very close to you, is so basely deceiving you. . . . You have let her go to your own as well as to her ruin, into the claws of a man who terrifies her, but who fascinates her by his flattering addresses. . . . When you see the dark man, who loves haunting your doors, have a good look at him. . . .
    Nothing but your nobility compels me to reveal this secret to you. And if you don't trust me, then have a look at the locket which your wife wears round her neck, and see whose portrait she wears in that locket near her heart.

YOUR EVEN UNKNOWN WELL-WISHER."

. . . .

. . . a playful idea flashed across my mind—to copy that letter . . . and to send it by post to Fiodor. . . . Next morning I posted it, and in the afternoon it was delivered to us. . . .
. . . After dinner . . . [Fiodor] went into his study. . . .
    I . . . asked Fiodor something to which he had to give an answer. But he kept a gloomy silence, and paced the room with heavy steps. I saw he was upset, and instantly I felt sorry. To break the silence I asked him: "Why are you so gloomy, Fedya?"
    Fiodor gave me an angry look, walked across the room a couple of times and came to a stop just facing me.
    "You wear a locket?" he asked in a choking voice.
    "I do."
    "Show it to me."
    "What for? You have seen it many times."
    "Show—me—the locket!" . . .
    I realized that my joke had gone too far, and in order to reassure him I began undoing the collar of my dress. But I had no time to

[1] *The Meaning of Shakespeare* (Chicago: University of Chicago Press, 1951; Phoenix edition, 1960), II, 89–92.

take the locket out. . . . He quickly rushed to me and caught my chain with all his strength. It was a thin chain. . . . It broke instantly, and the locket remained in my husband's hand. . . . I saw how his hands trembled, and the locket nearly slipped from them on to the table. . . . At last my husband opened the locket and found there—on one side the portrait of our little daughter, on the other—his own portrait. He was absolutely confused, and kept on looking at the portrait in silence.

. . . .

Here, then, is another case of an older and experienced man married to a younger wife, hardly able to believe, as other documents attest, that his happiness is real. This man is, moreover, by general consent one of the profoundest students of human nature that ever lived. . . . Yet, caught in the grip of ancestral jealousy, his wisdom vanishes as if it had never existed and he becomes as helpless as a child. . . .[1]

ARTHUR SEWELL [2] [1951]

There is . . . a significant separateness of "worlds" in *Othello*; it is the separateness of Othello's world from that to which all the other characters equally belong. . . . Iago's world is the world of Venice, to which all the Venetians were born and in which they were imagined. It is more than that. It is society as Shakespeare now presented it. The central recommendation of society, so conceived, is cynically summed up in Iago's "Put money in thy purse." It is a world in which soldiers compete for office and prestige. It is a world in which, as Emilia well knows, men will do each other's offices in the women's beds. It is a world in which lust flaunts its finery and is not abashed. It is a world, indeed, from which spirit has been drained, and all is measured by use and entertainment and position. It is a kingdom of means, not ends.

We do not judge this society by any standard to which an actual society might attain. We do not set against it an ideal society towards which an actual society might asymptotically move. In judging the society of this Venice, we make a judgment on the very nature of all society whatsoever. We see that this society is, in fact, representative of society in general; and that society in general sets up use against value, expediency against integrity, prestige against

[1] In addition to the excerpt by Goddard, see Dostoevsky's treatment of jealousy in *The Brothers Karamazov* (Book VIII, Chapter III) in which he alludes to Pushkin's statement that "Othello was not jealous, he was trustful."

[2] *Character and Society in Shakespeare* (Oxford: Clarendon Press, 1951), pp. 93–94.

principle, behaviour against moral being. In *Othello,* two worlds are set in opposition; the world set in time and inhabited by the Venetians; the world of the spirit, in terms of which we apprehend Othello. For this reason, in the bulk of the play, these Venetians are seen from the outside, they are seen as they behave; whereas Othello is seen from within, he is seen as he is.

F. R. LEAVIS [1] [1952]

The generally recognized peculiarity of *Othello* among the tragedies may be indicated by saying that it lends itself as no other of them does to the approach classically associated with Bradley's name: even *Othello* (it will be necessary to insist) is poetic drama, a dramatic poem, and not a psychological novel written in dramatic form and draped in poetry, but relevant discussion of its tragic significance will nevertheless be mainly a matter of character-analysis. It would, that is, have lent itself uniquely well to Bradley's approach if Bradley had made his approach consistently and with moderate intelligence. Actually, however, the section on *Othello* in *Shakespearean Tragedy* is more extravagant in misdirected scrupulosity than any of the others; it is, with a concentration of Bradley's comical solemnity, completely wrong-headed—grossly and palpably false to the evidence it offers to weigh.

. . . .

According to the version of *Othello* elaborated by Bradley the tragedy is the undoing of the noble Moor by the devilish cunning of Iago. Othello we are to see as a nearly faultless hero whose strength and virtue are turned against him. Othello and Desdemona, so far as their fate depended on their characters and untampered-with mutual relations, had every ground for expecting the happiness that romantic courtship had promised. It was external evil, the malice of the demi-devil, that turned a happy story of romantic love —of romantic lovers who were qualified to live happily ever after, so to speak—into a tragedy. This—it is the traditional version of *Othello* and has, moreover, the support of Coleridge—is to sentimentalize Shakespeare's tragedy and to displace its centre.

. . . .

. . . it is plain that what we should see in Iago's prompt success is not so much Iago's diabolic intellect as Othello's readiness to respond. Iago's power, in fact, in the temptation-scene is that he represents

[1] *The Common Pursuit* (Harmondsworth, Middlesex: Penguin Books Ltd., 1963), pp. 136–137, 140–141.

something that is in Othello—in Othello the husband of Desdemona: the essential traitor is within the gates. For if Shakespeare's Othello too is simple-minded, he is nevertheless more complex than Bradley's. Bradley's Othello is, rather, Othello's; it being an essential datum regarding the Shakespearean Othello that he has an ideal conception of himself.

The tragedy is inherent in the Othello-Desdemona relation, and Iago is a mechanism necessary for precipitating tragedy in a dramatic action.

ROBERT B. HEILMAN [1] [1956]

. . . Iago has defined his own role with wonderful explicitness:

> Make after him, poison his delight,
> Proclaim him in the streets. Incense her kinsmen,
> And though he in a fertile climate dwell,
> Plague him with flies. (I,i, 68–71)

Poison and *plague*: here, almost before the play is started, Iago announces his trademarks. The words are more than the chance verbal instruments of rancor; they inaugurate a poetic structure that is sustained throughout the play. For we are to see Iago administering poison and spreading a plague, and actually using such terms for his work. . . .

The early identification of Iago as a poisoner sets the state for another remarkable dramatic definition of evil: the poisoner as physician. . . . The montaging of the healer upon the poisoner not only effects a coalescence of moral opposites that defines chaos, but reminds us that in virtue of his knowledge every doctor contains the poisoner: a potion can mean life or death to the man who drinks it. Hence we have a universal paradigm of evil, not a period piece from the antique mart. Physicians are rarely poisoners; they are subject to more than usual moral imperatives regarding human life because they have more than usual power over life and death.

. . . .

[Iago] nurses his patient toward an incurable condition. But Iago's dual role is set forth with most effective shock when, under his goading, Othello has a kind of fit—a scene which we can now see in perspective. Just after Othello falls, Iago exclaims, "Work on, /My medicine, work! Thus credulous fools are caught" (IV,i, 45–46). This is the climax of the poetic structure of the physician-poisoner:

[1] *Magic in the Web* (Lexington, Kentucky: University of Kentucky Press, 1956), pp. 91–93.

the two functions coalesce as Iago uses *medicine,* the commonest word in the vocabulary of healing, to denote his poisoning of Othello's mind; to describe the conversion of order into disorder, he uses a word connoting the reduction of disorder to order. Repeatedly *Othello* presents the diabolical principle as a reversal of the human norms which guarantee ordinary safety in existence.

ALBERT GERARD [1] [1957]

Whereas Shakespeare had keyed Hamlet's intelligence to the highest possible pitch, he deliberately stressed Othello's lack of intellectual acumen, psychological insight, and even plain common sense. In the play, Othello's negroid physiognomy is simply the emblem of a difference that reaches down to the deepest levels of personality. If Hamlet is over-civilized, Othello is, in actual fact, what Iago says he is, a "barbarian" [I,iii, 364].

Othello's fundamental barbarousness becomes clear when we consider his religious beliefs. His superficial acceptance of Christianity should not blind us to his fundamental paganism. . . . [His] primitive elements receive poetic and dramatic shape in the aura of black magic which at times surrounds Othello. . . . The magic in *Othello* results from his acquiescence in obscure savage beliefs. It is an elemental force at work in the soul of the hero. It helps to build up the Moor as a primitive type.

Here again, we wonder why Shakespeare was attracted by such a hero. A twentieth-century dramatist might be interested in the clash of two cultures, which occurs in the mind of Othello. But though this aspect of the situation is not altogether ignored by Shakespeare, his main concern lies in another direction. The fact is that this tragedy of deception, self-deception, unjustified jealousy and criminal revenge demanded such a hero.

The crime-columns of the newspapers teach us that the people who murder their wives out of jealousy are generally mental defectives. Ordinary sensible people simply cannot believe that such a crime should deserve such a punishment. It was impossible for Shakespeare to take a subnormal type as a hero for his tragedy. Tennessee Williams could do it, I suppose, but not Shakespeare, because the Renaissance tradition required that tragedy should chronicle the actions of aristocratic characters. He might have chosen as his hero some nobleman with an inflated sense of honour, but then he probably could not have made him gullible enough to swallow Iago's lies. *And it is precisely the gullibility that is essential.*

[1] " 'Egregiously an Ass': The Dark Side of the Moor. A View of Othello's Mind," *Shakespeare Survey, 10* (1957), pp. 99–100.

Shakespeare was not intent on emulating Heywood's achievement of the year before in *A Woman Killed with Kindness*. *Othello* is not a tragedy of jealousy: it is a tragedy of *groundless* jealousy.

So, in Cinthio's tale, Shakespeare found reconciled with a maximum of credibility the requirements of Renaissance tragedy and the necessities of his own private purpose: a character with a high rank in society, with a noble heart, and with an under-developed mind. . . . We may say without exaggeration that Othello's lack of intellectual power is the basic element in his character.

BERNARD SPIVACK [1] [1958]

. . . When William Hazlitt described Iago as "an amateur of tragedy in real life," when Bradley noted as "a curious point of technique" with Shakespeare that Iago's "soliloquies . . . read almost like explanations offered to the audience," and when other critics observe the "histrionic" or "artistic" element in the performance, they all respond to a phenomenon whose real nature, although they do not quite discern it, is by now sufficiently familiar to us. It is once more the homiletic dramaturgy of the moral play, where personified evil demonstrated its destructive operation and preached its own exposure, addressing itself as intimately to its audience as any minister to his congregation or pedagogue to his pupils, with the difference that the dramatized lesson was made trenchant by satire and by action. This method reached its culmination in the Vice and descended from him to the line of villains he fathered. All of them manipulate their victims into comic or tragic confusion in order to exhibit the name and nature of villainy. It is, as we have seen, a declining method, and in Iago it is substantially diminished in its two principal features: the action loses as a demonstration what it gains as an organic plot, and the homily recedes before the enactment of the literal story. But although diminished it remains, exploited by the playwright at the height of his powers.

IRVING RIBNER [2] [1960]

Othello is of great potential virtue, but when he comes upon the scene he is, like the early Hamlet, as yet untried. In spite of his age he has not yet encountered the evil of the world. The play will be his baptism; he will encounter evil as Adam had encountered it, and like Adam he will fall, but in his own destruction he will learn

[1] *Shakespeare and the Allegory of Evil* (New York: Columbia University Press, 1958), pp. 436–437.

[2] *Patterns in Shakespearian Tragedy* (New York: Barnes & Noble, Inc., 1960), pp. 93–94, 112–113, 115.

the nature of evil. He will learn to distinguish true virtue from seeming virtue, and from his tragedy he will emerge the kind of man who is capable of salvation. Shakespeare says in the destruction of Othello, as in that of Hamlet, that true virtue and wisdom may come to man only through suffering, struggle and self-mastery. It is the tragedy of human life that this must be so.

. . . In *Othello* evil is an active force embodied in Iago. He is a dramatic symbol of evil whose function is to cause the downfall of Othello, and although Shakespeare endows him with an illusion of reality so supreme in its artistry that it has escaped analysis as thoroughly as that of Hamlet, in the larger symbolic design of the play he needs no specific motivation.

. . . .

Desdemona is endowed, like Othello and Iago, with the illusion of reality, but in the total scheme of the play she stands from first to last as an incarnation of self-sacrificing love. She is a reflection of Christ, who must die at the hands of man, but out of whose death may spring man's redemption.

. . . .

. . . The evil of her murder she will repay with forgiveness and mercy, out of evil creating good. Her unconquerable love for Othello will be his redemption.

Thus, although Othello dies accepting damnation as his just desert, Shakespeare by his careful delineation of Desdemona as a symbol of mercy has prepared the audience for the salvation of Othello in spite of all. Othello dies truly penitent. He takes the step which Claudius, in spite of his fears of damnation, cannot take. Othello destroys himself in an act of expiation, and his final words are a reminder to the audience of his union in death with the goodness he had tried to destroy:

> I kiss'd thee ere I killed thee: no way but this;
> Killing myself, to die upon a kiss. (V,ii, 358–359)

The audience knows that in his renunciation of evil, his penance and expiation, Othello has merited salvation.

. . . .

The tragedy of *Othello*, in its neatness and precision of construction, parallels more closely than any of Shakespeare's other plays what may be called the prototype of tragedy in Christian Europe, that of Adam in the garden of Eden. *Othello* expresses more perfectly than any of the other plays the paradox of the fortunate fall through which the Christian world could postulate a merciful and purposive God in spite of Adam's tragedy. The play is Christian in its symbolism and in the central intellectual proposition which shapes and controls the action, character and poetry of which it is comprised. *Othello* couches its universal propositions in terms of specific action and specific character, which in the speedy movement of the scenes retain an illusion of reality in spite of the logical inconsistencies which the scholar's study may reveal. It creates an emotional equivalent for its central idea and a tension between emotion and intellect which is the essence of tragedy. We participate fully in the horror which falls upon Othello, while rationally we are assured and seconded in our faith in divine order.

MARVIN ROSENBERG [1] [1961]

It is not necessary for us, as it was for the psychologist, to find in a man's childhood the conditions that make him fearful of emotion and drive him to seek omnipotence in fantasy and vindictiveness. For us, Iago had no childhood; he exists only as a more or less valid reflection of life in the dramatic art form. What is important here is that Shakespeare worked out dramatically how these things could be—how intimately related were the need for vindictive triumph and the need to deny positive feelings, how pervasive and powerful was the resulting misdirected hostility, how dangerously and poisonously it fumed beneath the surface when further compressed by the outward need to appear pleasant and subordinate.

It is no longer surprising that Shakespeare sensed complexities of human motivation that psychologists are still trying to explain. Freud long ago paid tribute to him for that. But it is interesting to see how deep his insight could go. For having shaped the true mental and emotional qualities of his "vindictive man," the playwright added a distinctive physical illness that plagued Iago savagely and one that, in his revenge fantasies, he hoped to fasten onto Othello.

The illness is common today—it is almost expected in those individuals who burn with resentment that they try to suppress. It feeds on internalized rage. In Iago it occurs when, out of the deep well of his self-contempt, he dredges up a fantasy with which to torture himself: the idea that Othello had sexual relations with Emilia:

> . . . The thought whereof
> Doth (like a poisonous mineral) gnaw my inwards . . .
> (II,i, 305–306)

[1] *The Masks of Othello* (Berkeley and Los Angeles: University of California Press, 1961), pp. 176–178.

Iago does, that is, burn inwardly from a familiar, severe functional disorder that eats a man away within when his nerves flay his stomach. He resembles a recognizable type of sufferer from that abrasion of the "inwards" that leads to painful ulceration. This "type" is the person who is driven, to quote one medical study, to evolve ". . . a life pattern of being self-sufficient, independent, or the 'lone-wolf.'" This pattern is commonly accompanied by "feelings of resentment and hostility." Case studies show that such persons frequently take out some of their aggressions on exploitable underlings, as an accompaniment to the aggressive fantasies they nurse toward persons they are unable to manipulate.

Iago, who is ceaselessly on fire with suppressed hostility against those he cannot openly exploit, represents the typical host for this gnawing "poisonous mineral" of an illness; if he mistakes its physiological nature, he knows well enough what causes it in him. A thought, a conceit, like his suspicion of Emilia's infidelity, is enough to set the sharp teeth biting at his gut; and it is precisely such a conceit that he hopes to feed Othello, for

> Dangerous conceits, are in their nature poisons
> Which
> . . . with a little act upon the blood,
> Burn like the mines of sulphur. (III,iii, 326–329)

Iago knew the feeling well. The imagery is so sharp that one wonders how well Shakespeare himself might have been acquainted with the problem. Certainly Renaissance psychologists knew its signs, little as they understood its physiology: thus, a late-sixteenth-century treatise explained: "But the envious body is constrained to bite on his bridle, to chew and to devoure his envy within himselfe and to lock up his owne miserie in the bottome of his heart, to the end it breake not foorth and shew it selve." Iago indeed chewed and devoured his envy within himself.

CONTEMPORARY CRITICISM OF *OTHELLO,*
A BIBLIOGRAPHY

1. A. C. Bradley, *"Othello," Shakespearean Tragedy*. London, 1904.
    This classic work is the beginning of modern Shakespearean criticism, freeing the study of Shakespeare from the historical approach of the nineteenth century and introducing universal considerations. Lecture Five discusses the control of the plot and the characters of Othello, noble but caught under the spell of Iago, and Desdemona. Lecture Six deals with Iago, who seems to be the bluff soldier, egotist,

with a strong will to power which he must test. Bradley does not accept Iago's stated motives for his evil and has been much criticized on this and several other points. Most agree, however, that this is an extremely stimulating work.

2. Lily B. Campbell, *"Othello:* A Tragedy of Jealousy," *Shakespeare's Tragic Heroes.* Cambridge, Eng., 1930; reprinted by Barnes & Noble, Inc., 1960.

This work as a whole deals with the relationship of Renaissance psychological theories to the tragedies of Shakespeare. The chapter on *Othello* contains a comparison of the play with Varchi's *The Blazon of Jealousie,* a sixteenth-century treatise. The interpretation of the play centers around the theme of jealousy in terms of what the passion meant to a Renaissance audience. Othello is a slave of the passion.

3. E. E. Stoll, *"Othello," Art and Artifice in Shakespeare.* Cambridge, Eng., 1933; reprinted by Barnes & Noble, Inc., 1962.

Stoll belongs to the school of "skeptical critics," and his thesis is that one cannot find realism in drama but must look instead for effect. He approaches the development of the play, and particularly Othello's change in character, in terms of prevalent dramatic conventions rather than in terms of realism and psychological validity. The book is a useful, but not entirely successful, rebuttal to Bradley and the "character critics."

4. Caroline F. E. Spurgeon, *Shakespeare's Imagery.* New York, 1935, pp. 335–338.

The book is a close analysis of prevailing images, and the brief section on *Othello* deals with the use and meaning of the animal and sea imagery.

5. Arthur Colby Sprague, *"Othello," Shakespeare and the Actors.* Cambridge, Mass., 1944.

This work deals with the history of the acting of the plays; the section on *Othello* is concerned particularly with the varying interpretations of the characters. Sprague pays special attention to stage business and production methods. Different acting interpretations of ambiguous passages aid in discovering the meanings of the passages.

6. Harley Granville-Barker, *Othello, Prefaces to Shakespeare,* II. London, 1945.

Beginning with a discussion of the changes made from the original story, Granville-Barker discusses the play scene by scene, and ends with interpretations of individual characters and a brief discussion of the imagery of the play. He sees the play as a tragedy without meaning, since he rejects the idea of Othello's salvation, and considers evil to have triumphed. Othello's jealousy is madness, since he did not have the seeds of it in his character. Granville-Barker's study is especially valued as coming from a man of the theater.

7. H. B. Charlton, *"Othello," Shakespearian Tragedy.* Cambridge, Eng., 1948.

This chapter is an analysis of the play according to the tradition of A. C. Bradley: Othello is the noble Moor victimized by Iago and guilty of being trusting and losing his self-control; Iago, however, is motivated from within, being in love with Desdemona, and is not a Satanic figure. Othello does not understand the Christianity he has adopted or the Venetians he lives among. His tragedy is the clash of the two traditions—the Venetian and the African, and is therefore not due to any chance encounter with Iago.

8. Hardin Craig, "The Great Trio," *An Interpretation of Shakespeare.* New York, 1948.

Craig approaches the play from the point of view that Shakespeare understood and believed in the perfect villain, as did other Elizabethans. He is interested in the conflict between will and conscience, and sees Othello as one who suffers from his virtues and is destroyed by his inability to recognize evil. The lie of Desdemona, seen here as perfect innocence, is considered the turning point of the drama.

9. G. Wilson Knight, "The *Othello* Music," *The Wheel of Fire.* Oxford, 1930.

Othello is a tragedy more particular in scope than the others, a story of intrigue, not a statement of universal values. This conclusion is reached by an analysis of Othello's metaphors, which, although lofty, are not taken by Knight as indicative of high questioning or seeking. Othello is caught between the divine Desdemona and the devilish Iago, and yields to Iago's evil. The author subjects the music symbolism to close analysis, and interprets it allegorically.

10. Richard Flatter, *The Moor of Venice.* London, 1950.

This is a close textual study of the play which emphasizes the importance of the Venetian setting and the part played by Brabantio. Critics have noted some unusual positions taken by Flatter: the belief that Othello is motivated by conviction, not jealousy; the analysis of Iago's character in terms of his constant self-dramatization; and the belief that Othello knows at the end he has been forgiven and regains his faith in human nature.

11. W. H. Clemen, *"Othello," The Development of Shakespeare's Imagery.* Cambridge, Mass., 1951.

This is a discussion of the play as a stage in the development of control and purpose in Shakespeare's imagery. In *Othello* imagery is used as a means of characterization. The imagery is discussed as it reveals character by means of characteristic word usages, different ways of referring to similar themes, and the time at which different kinds of imagery appear in the speeches of various characters. The imagery is a counterpoint to the action on the stage. Of particular importance is the animal imagery.

12. J. V. Cunningham, "Reason Panders Will," *Woe or Wonder: the Emotional Effect of Elizabethan Tragedy*. Denver, 1951.

The section on *Othello* is mainly an explication of the scene in which Iago tempts Othello to jealousy. The rationale of the scene is based, according to Cunningham, on the syllogism that either Iago or Desdemona is honest. Othello's experience inclines him to believe Iago; therefore his conversion is not just passion or a convention, but is possible by Iago's logic.

13. Harold C. Goddard, *"Othello," The Meaning of Shakespeare,* II. Chicago, 1951.

Goddard gives an unusual interpretation of Iago, seen as a slave at heart, pure intellect, an icy personality likened to the mass personality which perverts intelligence to the uses of war. Iago must have potentiality for good in order to pretend goodness, and so he is genuinely moved by Desdemona's kneeling to him.

14. Arthur Sewell, "Tragedy and 'The Kingdom of Ends'," *Character and Society in Shakespeare*. Oxford, 1951.

The tragedies are examples of society versus a single human being, and the character in the social order is carefully examined. Venice and the Venetians are co-conspirators with Iago, who represents the worst of civilized society. Othello is a spiritual man at odds with this society and destroyed by it.

15. G. R. Elliott, *The Flaming Minister*. Durham, N. C., 1953.

A scene-by-scene commentary in which the interrelationships of scenes are examined. The motif of *Othello* is pride, and character and plot are interpreted in the light of the workings of pride.

16. Virgil K. Whitaker, *"Othello, Macbeth,* and *King Lear," Shakespeare's Use of Learning*. San Marino, Calif., 1953.

Not a detailed study of the play, this interpretation emphasizes those points which indicate Shakespeare's thinking and which carry out the theme of the book, the study of sin in the individual. Othello represents rational good and Iago rational evil; Iago uses sensual imagery to change Othello's thinking from reason to passion. The climax of the play is an act of moral choice, and the basic sin is pride.

17. Robert B. Heilman, *Magic in the Web*. Lexington, Ky., 1956.

In an extremely thorough analysis Heilman considers all parts of the play in their relationships to each other. The play is a play about love and a poem about love at the same time. The jealousy of Iago is central to the tragedy, whereas Othello is confused and rather brutal. The main theme of the play is the various effects of and approaches to love. Of great use in this book are the notes at the end in which most of the best critics of *Othello* are cited and discussed.

18. Brents Stirling, "Reputation, Reputation, Reputation," *Unity in Shakespeare Tragedy*. New York, 1956.

Stirling examines the play in terms of the theme of reputation and honor. Othello's motivation is concern for his good name, which lends a ritual tone to his sacrifice of Desdemona. The author also discusses the symbolism of pride, light and dark, and the handkerchief.

19. Harold S. Wilson, *"Othello," On the Design of Shakespearian Tragedy*. Toronto, 1957.

The relationships among the tragedies are discussed in terms of thesis, antithesis, and synthesis, *Othello* and *Macbeth* being the antithesis of *Romeo and Juliet* and *Hamlet*. *Othello* is considered in terms of Christian thought as a part of the "order of faith."

20. Kenneth Muir, *"Othello," Shakespeare's Sources*. London, 1957.

Shakespeare may well have read the original story by Cinthio in Italian. Muir deals with the difference between the original and the Shakespearean version, and the significance of the changes made by Shakespeare.

21. Paul Siegel, *"Othello," Shakespearean Tragedy and the Elizabethan Compromise*. New York, 1957.

In a symbolical interpretation of the play, Siegel sees Iago as a devil and Desdemona as a Christ figure sacrificed in a ritual murder. Othello is a noble soul caught in the toils of one who is cynical and base. The symbolism of Venice and the handkerchief is also discussed.

22. D. A. Traversi, "The Mature Tragedies," *An Approach to Shakespeare*, 2nd ed. Glasgow, 1957.

Traversi sees the play in terms of the paradoxical difference in the imagery and emotions of Othello and Iago. Othello is passionate, but his imagery is cold; Iago is passionless, but his imagery is sensual. Thus the plot resolves into a conflict between Othello and Iago, and Othello's purity of love is poisoned. His naïve self-love has allowed it to be poisoned.

23. Bernard Spivack, *Shakespeare and the Allegory of Evil.* New York, 1958.

In this study of villains and villainy, Iago is subjected to a penetrating analysis, particularly in terms of his relationship to the Vice character in the morality plays.

24. Irving Ribner, "The Pattern of Moral Choice: *Othello,*" *Patterns of Shakespearian Tragedy.* London and New York, 1960.

Ribner's thesis stresses the non-naturalism of the Elizabethan theater, the symbolic tradition which came from the morality plays. To the Elizabethans, evil was an active force which needed no motivation. In support of this point of view, Ribner explicates several significant passages and discusses the functions of various characters. He considers the play the prototype of Christian tragedy and believes that Othello is redeemed by his self-realization.

25. J. A. Bryant, *"Othello," Hippolyta's View: Some Christian Aspects of Shakespeare's Plays.* Lexington, Ky., 1961.

Finding Biblical references in the play, Bryant assigns the characters symbolic values in Christian terms. Iago is a Satanic figure; Desdemona represents Othello's possibilities of salvation; Cassio is Adam; and Othello is God. The symbolism is compared with that of Milton's *Paradise Lost,* but the critic acknowledges that the story is mainly that of the Moor. For a rebuttal of the theory, see Roland Mushat Frye, *Shakespeare and Christian Doctrine* (Princeton, New Jersey, 1963).

26. Marvin Rosenberg, *The Masks of Othello.* Berkeley and Los Angeles, 1961.

This is a stage history of the play, a discussion of the actors and critics in various periods and their conceptions of the production and interpretation of the play. The section of the book entitled *"Othello* and the Critics" contains much useful summary of critical material, as well as an illuminating interpretation of the play as something to be read.

7. Staging and Production

Othello has provoked violent emotions in its audiences throughout its long history. Perhaps because it is a domestic tragedy, microcosmic in scope, it has been taken personally by actors and witnesses alike; the history of its performances is filled with incidents of screaming, swooning, and audience participation. Because of the violence of these reactions, the play presents peculiar problems to the actor, problems which have been differently approached in each age, and which are akin to the critical interpretations of the play.

Our knowledge of the early performances is limited by the lack of contemporary accounts: research has indicated that *Othello* was probably first performed in 1604 by Shakespeare's own company. In days when plays were seldom performed repeatedly, *Othello* was honored by several performances within the lifetime of the author, one performance contributing to the celebration of the marriage of Princess Elizabeth in 1612. During this period, and for several years after Shakespeare's death, the part of Othello was taken by Richard Burbage, the most famous tragedian of the age. There is no record of how the play was performed, how the parts were interpreted, or even how the play was received; we may surmise, however, that it was popular with Shakespeare's contemporaries, since it was so often performed.

More informative accounts of performances of *Othello* begin to appear toward the end of the seventeenth century, when the Restoration of the English monarchy restored also the popularity of the stage as an art. Samuel Pepys twice notes in his diary that he attended performances in which he saw Mrs. Hughes, probably the first woman to appear on the English stage, take the part of Desdemona. Plays were evidently performed with great realism and taken very seriously in this period, and Pepys records an incidence of a woman nearby fainting at the murder of Desdemona. There is still no specific information about the way in which actors interpreted their parts. According to Marvin Rosenberg,[1] however, *Othello* was probably performed with an emphasis on the sexual imagery and particularly the bawdy humor of Iago; this was what appealed to the Restoration.

As the seventeenth century advanced, and the aged Burt as Othello gave way to Betterton, changes crept into the acting of *Othello*. The changes began as an increasing classicism and sense of decorum emerged in the literature and criticism of the period. Othello became more refined, more like the classic hero, and Desdemona became more of a gentlewoman, in eighteenth-century terms. An acting copy of the play, which has come to us from the Smock Alley theater in Dublin, shows subtle changes in the text and deletions of Othello's cruder or less heroic speeches such as "Set on thy wife to observe," which would be considered unbecoming to a great warrior. Betterton was extremely successful in the role; and Sir Richard Steele praised him highly in a *Tatler* essay (no. 167, Thursday, May 4, 1710),

---

[1] This account owes much to Rosenberg's excellent survey, *The Masks of Othello* (Berkeley and Los Angeles, 1961).

and seemed to reflect the prevailing opinion, for Betterton played Othello from 1683 to 1709. A succession of Othellos followed, about whose style we know little: Barton Booth played the part until 1727; Quin until 1751; Sheridan was not particularly good in the part in 1761.

Throughout this period more and more cuts were being made in the text of the play, until Othello's tale of cannibals was no longer heard, nor could he fall into a trance, and his "but yet the pity of it, Iago" could not show hesitancy on the part of a stern hero. It was customary for the noble Moor to wear the uniform of a British officer, even to a white wig. Yet the play was successful and performed at least once nearly every year of the eighteenth century. About mid-century David Garrick, the friend of Samuel Johnson and famous actor whose new, more violently emotional acting style was becoming popular, attempted the role. After his success as Macbeth, the part seemed a certain triumph for him, and he daringly restored some of the cut scenes. But Garrick was short in stature, and too tempestuous in emotion; in turban and blackface he reminded Quin of a small Negro slave in a painting by Hogarth, and Quin demolished the characterization by inquiring nastily after Garrick's teakettle. So the century's most famous actor failed in the role. It remained for Spranger Barry to reconcile the two extremes, Quin's coldness with Garrick's storminess, to achieve a controlled and dignified but passionate Moor.

If the censoring of the play complicated the interpretation of Othello's part, it made the acting of Iago even more difficult. Modern critics attach great importance to Iago's use of sexual imagery, his obsession with the sexual act, and this was cut from the acting editions of *Othello* in the eighteenth century. To play the part without this imagery and still provide a motivation for the character's evil must have placed an almost intolerable burden upon the actor, and indeed records of the time show few entirely successful Iagos. Desdemona was made more of a great lady in this period, and was played as such by Mrs. Siddons, who evoked tremendous sympathy from her audience.

In the nineteenth century even more censoring was in store for the play. Bowdler, the infamous censor who produced a suitable "family" Shakespeare in the early part of the century, was only one of many such expurgators and self-appointed moralists who revised Shakespeare. The actors followed suit, with only an occasional protest, for this was an age of propriety. John Philip Kemble, with Mrs. Siddons as Desdemona, was a cold, mysterious Othello in the early years; he was replaced by Edmund Kean, who overcame his short height to become the most famous Othello of them all. Both Keats and Hazlitt remember with pleasure and awe the strength of Kean's performance.

Kean played the part into the thirties, once defying an angry audience which was protesting against him for his adultery conviction, and his last performance ended in collapse at the end of the third act.

Perhaps because of the extreme reticence of the text, the Othellos of the mid-nineteenth century tended toward exaggerated acting styles. Macready, a rather imprecise Moor, competed with Kean for the role, but was never quite happy with it; he preferred the part of Macbeth, in which he excelled. Salvini, who played the part in Italian, was the sensation of the age, acting with such fury that his Desdemonas, dragged about the stage by the hair, became rebellious. Indeed the part of Desdemona was so eclipsed and so dangerous in this period that many actresses refused it altogether. Salvini's violence was appealing and widely acclaimed, but some critics and audiences preferred the more restrained acting of Edwin Booth. Booth was a very successful Othello, though he did not, like Salvini, seize Iago by the throat, but confined his activity on the stage to heartrending groans and weeping. Booth's acting was thoroughly purged of all obscenities, even to the elimination of the word "whore," but he brought new insight into the interpretation of the character by his emphasis on the sacrificial murder of Desdemona. Extremely detailed accounts of both actors' interpretations exist and are of interest to scholars in their studies of the meaning of the play.

Edwin Forrest, the first American tragedian to achieve international renown, was fated to play a parallel role in his own life. Tormented by doubts about his own wife's fidelity, he played the Moor with a passion and intensity—from the noble hero to the driven beast—which, according to contemporary accounts, verged on madness. His characterization was perhaps marred by his close identification with the role, but he contributed to the conception of Othello's great dignity and depth of agony. Other actors achieved some success in the part, but these three, Salvini with his passion, Booth with his subtlety, and Forrest with his pitiableness, probably contributed most to the role.

The same group of actors were also reasonably successful in the role of Iago in spite of a decimated text. In particular they managed to maintain the balance between coarseness and refinement which seems to be necessary to the stage version of the role. There arose with Kean the problem of the light-hearted villain which has plagued actors ever since, the bawdy humor of the part tempting them to play it for laughs. Kean apparently went too far, in the opinion of many, in making Iago the jovial, careless prankster. It remained for better Iagos to use the spirited dialogue as a mask for the inner villainy of the man. Interestingly enough, the better Iagos were often actors who had not achieved great success as Othello. Macready was one of these, playing cat and mouse games with Othello in the guise of the honest soldier; Irving and Fechter, neither better than adequate Othellos, also contributed to the characterization of Iago, the former by the fascination of the gay villain, the latter by his emphasis on Iago's hypocrisy.

The character of Desdemona underwent deep analysis in the nineteenth century, though the part was reduced by censoring to practically nothing. Some few Desdemonas, notably Helen Faucit and Ellen Terry, managed to evoke the pity which was an important part of the play in the eighteenth century. Ellen Terry commented in lectures that she considered Desdemona to be a strong woman, and she played the part so convincingly that she brought tears to Irving's eyes when, as Desdemona, she pleaded with him as Iago to help her win Othello back.

The end of the century saw actors such as Barry Sullivan, Forbes Robertson, and Oscar Asche in the role of Othello, but apparently they added nothing new to the characterization. In the twentieth century experimental stagings of the play have been tried, such as Laurence Olivier's production in which a homosexual basis for Iago's evil was explored. The production was a failure, according to critics, for Olivier fell into the trap of playing Iago as too jovial a character, thereby leaving him with no apparent motivation for his evil. A summary of the criticism of twentieth-century productions indicates this, with the inability of some Othellos to dominate the play, as the major cause of failure in inspiration in the acting of the play. The most noteworthy Othello has been Paul Robeson, whose calm dignity in the part was praised highly; yet his characterization was found wanting in grandeur, and he was at times too conscious of his own race to give the part universality. The twentieth century seems to be groping still for an actor to play the part with the proper amounts of dignity and passion, though a 1964 production with Olivier as Othello was widely acclaimed.

8. Suggestions and Questions for Study, Review, and Essay Topics

Many of the questions which follow will require only a careful reading of the text of *Othello* and familiarity with it for adequate answers. Others will involve a comparison of pertinent passages in the play with each other and with the views of various critics (quoted in this volume) about them. Some questions will lead the reader and student to original sources and to materials not available in the present book.

Theme, Setting, Imagery

1. Could the first act of *Othello* be omitted without any loss to the play as Samuel Johnson asserts? What would be lost in not having directly presented the character of Brabantio, the Venetian setting, and the council scene in which the two lovers defend their marriage?

2. Do most of the crucial scenes in *Othello* take place at night or in daytime? With what effect on the atmosphere of the play?

3. Think of the action of *Othello* occurring only during the so-called slow time (see Part II, Chapter III) or only during the fast time. What problems arise in either case (1) in the plot (e.g., the presence of Lodovico, Cassio's relations with Bianca) and (2) in characterization, especially of Othello and Desdemona?

4. Explain clearly why *Othello* is a domestic tragedy.

5. Wolfgang Clemen says that Othello is characterized by dynamic imagery and Iago by static imagery. Collect enough examples in the play to confirm him. Drawing on your general knowledge of Coleridge, can you point out any connection between his ideas on the imagination and Clemen's two kinds of imagery?

6. Can you argue that powerful imagery has as much dramatic effect on the audience as striking action? Support your answer with examples from *Othello*.

7. How convincing is Marvin Rosenberg's interpretation of Iago? Both he and Robert B. Heilman pay much attention to the imagery connected with illness. Compare their observations and conclusions. Are they successful in dealing with character through imagery?

8. Select one theme of the imagery mentioned in Part II, Chapter IV, which has not been discussed in this book and collect as many examples as you can find in the play (e.g., economics, stealing). Is the cumulative effect of images on this theme powerful enough to affect the atmosphere of whole scenes? Of the entire play?

9. Write an essay discussing the imagery used by any one character.

Characterization

1. When Iago says "an erring barbarian and a supersubtle Venetian," he is evidently contending that Othello and Desdemona are in some sense opposites. Explain his meaning as fully as you can. Do you think he is putting his finger on the primary cause of the tragedy which is to follow?

2. Which motives does Iago give himself for his actions? Why is it that critics like Samuel Taylor Coleridge and Harley Granville-

Barker call him "motiveless" and critics such as William Hazlitt, Robert B. Heilman, and Marvin Rosenberg credit him with motives but differ as to what they are?

3. How does Othello's attitude toward love change throughout the play? Is his view of love ever *identical* with that of Iago?

4. Of the three main characters, Desdemona speaks the fewest lines, yet her qualities of courage, selfless devotion, and chastity are made perfectly clear to the audience. How is this accomplished?

5. How is Iago so successful in maintaining his guise of honesty to the main characters of the play? At what moment in the play does the audience begin to suspect that he is evil? How does his language figure in this?

6. Some critics have found it difficult to accept the psychological soundness of Othello's sudden belief in Desdemona's infidelity. Can you explain this change in terms of his trustfulness, self-deception, and simplicity of character?

7. How does Othello's imagination contribute to his breakdown? Cf. the critical excerpt of Wolfgang Clemen.

8. Are Iago's views of the natures of his wife Emilia, Cassio, Othello, and Desdemona accurate? If not, how does he manage to control them? Show how his downfall is the result of an ultimate lack of understanding of these characters.

9. Was it in the nature of Othello to be jealous, or was he forced to be jealous, against his better nature, by the machinations of Iago? What does evidence from the play seem to indicate? What do A. C. Bradley and Leo Kirschbaum have to say on the subject?

10. Evaluate Irving Ribner's interpretation of Desdemona in the play. Can you justify this?

11. Does the wittiness and apparent good-heartedness of Iago add to or detract from his characterization as an extremely evil person?

12. How does the critical excerpt from Harold Goddard's *The Meaning of Shakespeare* bear on the interpretation of Othello's character? After reading this excerpt, what comment would you make on the criticism of Gerard?

13. Roderigo is the only person until Act V to whom Iago willingly reveals his evil side. What does this indicate about Roderigo's character?

14. Although Brabantio appears only in Act I, we are forcibly reminded of his misgivings several times throughout the play. Point out these occasions. His death is reported in the final scene of Act V; what is the dramatic irony here?

15. Are Cassio and Roderigo well-developed characters? What is the importance of Cassio at the play's end?

16. Is such a character as Bianca necessary to the play? How does

the confusion of her identity with that of Desdemona intensify the horror of the play?

17. Can you reconcile Emilia's lie to the distraught Desdemona about the stolen handkerchief and her impassioned defense of Desdemona in the final scene?

18. Write an essay in which you describe (with evidence) one character as he might appear in the eyes of another (e.g., Iago as seen by Othello; Cassio as seen by Othello; Desdemona as seen by Emilia).

Staging, Production

1. What changes did Shakespeare make in his source; and how did his alterations enhance the theatrical effectiveness of the three main characters in the play (Othello, Iago, Desdemona)?

2. After reading the following modern critics, explain how each of them would picture Othello in Act V if he were producing the play: Leo Kirschbaum, Bernard Spivack, and Albert Gerard. Can you account for their different interpretations of the character?

3. Read the temptation scene (III,iii) leaving out the passage where Othello falls in a trance; also, the willow scene (IV,iii). These passages were usually omitted in Victorian productions. How do they alter the characterization of Othello and Desdemona?

4. Could *Othello* be produced effectively in modern dress? Explain the advantages. What scenes or lines, if any, should be cut?

5. How has the part of Desdemona been interpreted traditionally, especially in the nineteenth century? Could she be interpreted as a flawed character, as some critics have suggested? If so, how would this part be acted?

6. How were the characters made to conform to the idea of decorum in the eighteenth century?

7. Why have the intellectual Othellos and the too-jovial Iagos failed on the stage? What seems to be the standard stage interpretation of each of these characters?

8. How do the modern conceptions of Othello and Iago differ from those of the Restoration? The eighteenth century? The Victorian period? Account for the differences in terms of staging and production.

9. Can unorthodox or untraditional interpretations of *Othello* be justified? (For example, Sir Laurence Olivier's homosexual interpretation of Iago on the stage.)

10. Does Irving Ribner's understanding of the three main characters lend itself to a successful and dramatic production of *Othello*? If no, explain. If so, explain how his ideas might affect the performance of these roles.

11. Is the temptation scene more effective when Othello is portrayed (1) as highly emotional, easily moved to jealousy, or (2) as restrained and slow to credit Iago's insinuations? In each case, how would the character of Iago have to be played?

12. Can you add any reasons to the ones given at the end of *Staging and Production* as to why there have been no inspiring modern Othellos?

13. Write detailed advice to an actor playing Iago (or to one playing Othello) in the temptation scene.

Criticism and Interpretation

1. Thomas Rymer was a critic of strong and, at first glance, absurd opinions. (Macaulay called him the worst critic who ever lived.) Can you account for his statements in terms of rational critical doctrine? Rymer wrote only three quarters of a century after Shakespeare. Why isn't he more sympathetic to the dramatist than he is?

2. Although Leo Kirschbaum and Irving Ribner are present-day scholars, their views of the character of Othello differ markedly. Is it possible to accept both views, or does one exclude the other? What does your answer imply about the nature of literature?

3. How do the following critics' views on Othello's race differ: Mary Preston, H. B. Charlton, A. C. Bradley, Albert Gerard? How might an actor's interpretation of Othello alter if he took these views seriously?

4. Which flaws do the following critics attribute to Othello as a result of his behavior at the end of the play: T. S. Eliot, Robert B. Heilman, Leo Kirschbaum?

5. E. E. Stoll calls upon the dramatic conventions of Shakespeare's day to explain Othello's character; Albert Gerard asserts that Othello's character is dictated by the dramatic requirements of the play. Is there any affinity between their views? Is either interpretation entirely satisfactory? How can their interpretations be said to contrast with those of Bradley and Coleridge?

6. List the different approaches to the play made by the critics in this book. Which approaches seem more satisfactory? Less satisfactory? Do the less satisfactory approaches add anything to your understanding of the play?

7. Which character has given rise to the greater range of critical interpretation—Iago or Othello? Why is this character more puzzling, or stimulating, to the critics?

8. Read fully one of the books excerpted in this section and write a review of it, describing its point of view and assessing its persuasiveness and its importance.

Miscellaneous

1. What features make *Othello* an especially powerful play? In what respects would it be more powerful to the spectator than to the reader?
2. Compare *Othello* with some other Shakespearean tragedy. Apart from their greatness, how would you know that they were written by the same author?
3. In what ways is *Othello* only a limited masterpiece (compared with Shakespeare's other great plays)? In what respect is it almost uniquely strong?
4. Does the "universal significance" of the tragedy suffer from the fact that its hero is less gifted intellectually than Hamlet, or less important than King Lear?
5. Is this a play you wish to read or see a second time? What qualities of the play might you miss in a first exposure to it?
6. Is the tragedy of the play inevitable? What effect would inevitability have upon your enjoyment of a second performance?
7. What lessons, if any, does *Othello* hold for us? (Cf. Thomas Rymer).
8. As far as Iago is concerned, this is a revenge play. If you know any other early revenge play, write an essay comparing it with *Othello*.

PART THREE: HISTORICAL BACKGROUND[1]

1. Beginning and development of English Drama

When churchmen began arranging Scripture readings and chants in the form of conversation, they laid the foundations of drama in medieval Europe and England. One of the earliest of these dialogues exists as a fragment known as the *Quem Quaeritis* ("Whom Seek Ye?") trope. The words are in Latin; the scene is the tomb of the resurrected Christ on Easter morning; the dialogue is that of the women and the angel at the open tomb.

Such attempts to enlighten and enliven the presentation of Scripture proved increasingly popular with the people, the majority of whom were illiterate. Gradually these simple dramatic arrangements, which were often a part of the church service itself, separated themselves from the divine offices. Writers translated them from Latin into English in order that more people could understand and enjoy them. Finally, the plays left the sanctuary and became dramatic entertainment in their own right.

Mystery Plays

The next step in the growth of native English drama was the mystery play.[2] Scholars do not know exactly when plays of this type first appeared, but Professor Hardin Craig has shown that people in the west of England probably saw them performed as early as the second quarter of the fourteenth century.

In the beginning the Church prepared and sponsored mystery plays, each of which portrayed a specific incident or "mystery" of Biblical history. The purpose was to depict highlights of the entire Bible through a series of graphic scenes.

These plays were so entertaining and the demand for them was so great that production rapidly exceeded the resources of the Church. Consequently, the trade guilds in the more important towns of England assumed responsibility for their production.

[1] This section was prepared by J. Wilson McCutchan, General Editor of Shakespeare Focus Books, and also appears in *Macbeth: A Complete Guide to the Play*.

[2] Although there is a technical distinction between a *mystery* play and a *miracle* play, the former dramatizing an episode from Scripture and the latter dealing with some incident in the life of a saint, many writers use the terms interchangeably.

Typically the guilds presented mystery plays in a cycle which told Old Testament and New Testament history in a series, or sequence, of short dramatic episodes. A cycle might begin with the Creation of Man and end with the Day of Judgment. Within these limits the plays covered a variety of Biblical events. Among the most popular from the Old Testament were the Expulsion of Adam and Eve from Eden, the Murder of Abel, Noah's Flood, the Sacrifice of Isaac. From the New Testament period greatest emphasis fell on incidents in the story of Christ: the Annunciation, the Shepherds, the Wise Men, the Flight into Egypt, Herod's Slaughter of the Innocents, Mary Magdalene's Washing of Christ's Feet, the Last Supper, the Resurrection.

Guilds often sponsored and produced plays which had some relationship to their respective trades or to their patron saints. For example, in Chester the Water Carriers staged the Deluge; in York the Shipwrights presented the Building of the Ark, and the Goldsmiths gave the Adoration of the Magi; in both towns the Bakers enacted the Last Supper.

Each guild prepared a wagon to serve as the acting area. On the day when the cycle began, wagon number one would come to the first open square or major street intersection of the town. Here it stopped, and the cast presented its play. As soon as this play ended, the wagon (or pageant) moved to the next "station," where the actors repeated the performance. While this was taking place wagon number two arrived at "station" number one. Spectators had the option of taking a fixed position and watching the entire cycle pass before them, or they could accompany any given wagon, see this play two or more times, and then wait for subsequent wagons to appear.

Although many cycles of mystery plays existed in medieval England, only four survive in varying degrees of completeness. These are the York, Chester, Wakefield (or Towneley), and Hegge (sometimes misleadingly called Coventry) plays. Each cycle has certain features which distinguish it from the others. Of greatest interest to lovers of drama is the Wakefield Cycle, in which the blending of Biblical incident and comedy and the skill of the unknown poet combine to make better drama than that characteristic of the other cycles. Notable among sporadic or non-cycle mystery plays [1] is the Brome *Abraham and Isaac*. Technically comic because of its fortunate ending for the two principal characters, this play comes closest to tragedy of all pre-Elizabethan drama.

As the mystery play flourished, writers emphasized comedy and

---

[1] Many scholars believe that these occasional plays may well be surviving units from lost cycles.

farce at the expense of the Biblical narrative. These added elements, although they increased the dramatic value and appeal of the plays, obscured the purpose which had led to their production. Eventually the Church and the guilds abandoned their encouragement and support of mystery cycles.

Before the mystery play went out of vogue, however, it made several valuable contributions to the development of English drama. Audiences became accustomed to the mingling of human and supernatural characters; they came to expect and to demand a certain amount of comic incident, even in the most serious and sacred situations; they developed a power to project themselves to faraway places with the aid of simple stage properties and conventional costumes.

Morality Plays

When the mystery play began to wane in its appeal, the morality play supplanted it. It would be incorrect to suppose that the mystery play stopped, suddenly to be replaced by the morality. Actually, *The Castle of Perseverance* (*c.* 1405–1425), which is the earliest complete morality play extant, appeared before mystery plays reached their peak in the fifteenth century. These two forms, the mystery and the morality, existed concurrently; the mystery play started sooner, and the morality reached the zenith of its popularity later and lasted longer. Whereas mystery plays were amateur productions, moralities formed the repertory of small bands of strolling players. These professional actors moved from town to town with their own staging, props, and costumes, and depended on modest fees and contributions for their livelihood.

Morality plays attempted to teach a lesson or moral. They showed vices and virtues in conflict with each other for possession of the soul of Man. Almost all morality plays fall into two broad classes: full-scope moralities (e.g., *The Castle of Perservance*) which dramatize the ethical struggle of man throughout life, and limited-scope moralities (e.g., *Everyman*) which depict this struggle at one special point or time in man's life. Basically, morality plays were allegorical, and the most striking feature of their allegory was the personification of abstract forces and qualities as characters, of whom the most prominent as groups were the Seven Deadly Sins and their opposing Virtues.

Originally theological in their allegory, morality plays grew more and more secular in their emphasis. By the middle of the sixteenth century, Avarice, who appeared as a Deadly Sin in the early moralities, became a typical usurer, land-grabber, or forecloser of mortgages; Pride, often the leader of the Deadly Sins, changed into a class-conscious aristocrat or haughty churchman or social dandy.

During the first half of the sixteenth century writers began using moralities for the encouragement of education, for attacks on social abuses, for political propaganda, and as weapons in religious controversy. Rapidly the number of concrete, flesh-and-blood characters increased until they outnumbered the abstractions which had once dominated the morality stage.

In much the same way as it had crept into the narrative of the mystery play, comedy began to usurp the didactic or teaching function of the morality. Most popular of all morality roles was the Vice. In the beginning an awesome combination of all sins and vicious qualities, this character became a conventional clown and practical jokester. He often dressed in beggar's clothing, carried a wooden sword and coiled rope, and dashed about, tripping other characters and making scurrilous wisecracks. The Vice was indispensable to the morality play, and many scholars have demonstrated that he was the direct dramatic ancestor of the Elizabethan Clown or Fool.[1]

One of the favorite endings for morality plays was a scene in which the Devil carried the Vice on his back to Hell. Stages had trapdoors which opened at the appropriate moment, permitting flames and smoke to belch forth. Into this opening the Devil and Vice could vanish without physical harm to themselves. In the same way as the Vice became the Clown of later drama, this Hell's Mouth of the morality stage became the trapdoor which was a feature of the Elizabethan theater.

Among several conventional characters which Elizabethan drama inherited from the morality were the stupid constable, the heavy-drinking and thick-speaking Fleming, and the itinerant vagabond and ballad-monger.

Interludes

Last of the important forms of native English drama was the interlude, a one-act combination of morality play and comedy, which emerged before the morality play lost its popularity and continued well into the reign of Elizabeth. In fact, many interludes could pass for either moralities or comedies, depending on the emphasis which the reader places on them.

Because the word "interlude" comes from two Latin words, *inter* (between) and *ludus* (play), some scholars believe that companies may have used them as diversions or entertainments between acts of longer plays. Another theory is that wealthy people arranged for the production of interludes between courses of elaborate banquets

---

[1] For a discussion of possible influences of the Vice on villains in Elizabethan drama, see Bernard Spivack, *Shakespeare and the Allegory of Evil* (New York: Columbia University Press, 1958).

or state dinners, in much the same way as expensive restaurants and nightclubs provide floor shows today.[1]

In any event, the majority of interludes provide for "doubling." Writers carefully planned their dialogue so that four or six actors could play as many as twelve or sixteen parts without meeting themselves on the stage. Doubling has continued in the theater ever since, especially among stock or traveling companies.

Summary

Through this brief review, the reader can see that Elizabethan playwrights found many features of native drama ready for adaptation in the more elaborate comedies and tragedies of the last quarter of the sixteenth century. In precisely the same manner, audiences were already familiar with many character types and stage conventions which they were to see in the Theatre, the Curtain, the Globe, and other public playhouses.

2. England and London, 1558–1612

When Elizabeth I ascended the throne of England in 1558, she inherited responsibilities and problems which would have challenged the vigor and resourcefulness of her grandfather, Henry VII, who had established the Tudor dynasty after defeating Richard III on Bosworth Field in 1485. Elizabeth's half-brother, Edward VI, had died in 1553, while still a minor. Her older half-sister, Mary, who succeeded him, for five years had striven energetically and devoutly to restore England to the Roman Catholic faith and had married Philip II of Spain.

Continental rivalries, focused in Spain, beset Elizabeth and threatened to engulf her; internal jealousies and intrigues surrounded her. Her father, Henry VIII, had left England in economic difficulties which Edward and Mary had done little to remedy during their short reigns. Ambitious noblemen and politicians were eager to use their professed loyalty for their personal advantage. Until her execution in 1587, Mary, Queen of Scots (heir to the throne according to the Catholic belief that Elizabeth was illegitimate) posed as

[1] E. K. Chambers in *The Mediaeval Stage,* 2 vols. (New York: Oxford University Press, 1903), II, 181–183, *passim,* questions both of these interpretations and suggests that the word "interlude" connotes "a *ludus* carried on between *(inter)* two or more performers; in fact, a *ludus* in dialogue."

a constant menace to Elizabeth's security. Wary and wise beyond her years, Elizabeth carefully and persistently maintained and strengthened her position.

Whatever Elizabeth's personal beliefs and inclinations may have been, necessity frequently compelled her to employ devious and seemingly capricious methods of government. Contrary to contemporaneous poetic descriptions of her beauty and the grandeur of her court, Elizabeth was as homely in appearance as her character was frugal and stingy. Peace, nominal if not actual, with foreign powers was politically desirable; economically it was mandatory. Wars cost money; money depended on parliament's voting heavier taxes; a parliament convening to levy taxes could enact other legislation, some of which might not be favorable to the queen.

Consequently, Elizabeth found it expedient to rely on her peerage for administrative advice and executive action. To an uncanny degree she learned how to play each nobleman against his fellows, skillfully keeping each from acquiring too much power and influence. In according her peers honor and privilege and at the same time checking their ambition and even bankrupting them, she was shrewd, knowing, and ruthless. The Earl of Leicester, for example, found that commanding his queen's troops in the Low Countries demanded not only risking his life but also mortgaging much of his own private property in order to pay his soldiers.

In the eyes of the masses Elizabeth was the Virgin Queen who had chosen England as her spouse in preference to a personal marriage. In encouraging this concept she expected and received enthusiastic support from poets, playwrights, and courtiers. Writers and portraitists alike depicted her as Diana, goddess of the hunt and of chastity. However pleasing or secretly amusing such flattery may have been to the queen, she was astute enough to appreciate its value as propaganda, and she demanded it although her displeasure when she failed to receive it was greater than her reward when she did.

Throughout most of her reign Elizabeth stood as the champion and defender of Protestantism. Historians may disagree on the extent to which Elizabeth accepted or preferred Reformed dogma. The fact remains that her claim to England's throne rested on the sanction and authority of the Church of England. Roman Catholic Europe denied the legitimacy of her birth and the right of her succession.

Elizabeth's business sense and keen political judgment made her aware of the importance of annoying the Spaniards and maintaining direct contacts with the New World. While backing Drake, Hawkins, Frobisher, and others, she officially reprimanded them for their raids on Spanish treasure ships and establishment. Not until the destruc-

tion of the Armada in 1588 could Elizabeth and her fellow country-
men disregard the immediate threat of Spanish invasion.

How far Elizabeth molded her age and how far she was an acces-
sory to the times it is useless to inquire. Energetic, intelligent, and
forceful, as a woman she had to delegate many responsibilities to
her cabinet and male advisers. The majority of these served her
well and faithfully. Perhaps the era was greater than the individuals
who lived in it. Together, the times and the persons produced one
of the golden periods of English history and of English letters.

In general, one would describe Elizabeth's resign as prosperous.
Explorations overseas broadened the horizons of Elizabethans, and
Englishmen were becoming conscious that they were citizens of an
independent state which was becoming a world power. Playwrights
eagerly capitalized on this awareness in their dramatization of na-
tional history. Although the difference between the very wealthy
and the very poor was still great, the middle classes of craftsmen,
merchants, and professional men were steadily acquiring jurisdic-
tion and authority. Social distinctions were sharp and important,
but an individual with brains, imagination, and courage could win
advancement.

This union of relative peace and prosperity was favorable to
creative writing. Whether a writer lived on the patronage of some
wealthy sponsor or derived his income from penny admissions to the
theater, someone had to pay the cost. It is dangerous to generalize
about social, economic, and political progress and its relationship to
literature and other arts, but the outburst of Elizabethan poetry and
prose is a striking contrast to the relatively barren years of the fifteenth century when England suffered from the Wars of the Roses.
Shakespeare seems to have been aware of this, for consistently
throughout his chronicle plays he emphasizes the tragedy of internal
dissension and revolution.

> This England never did, nor never shall,
> Lie at the proud foot of a conqueror
> But when it first did help to wound itself.
> . . . .
> . . .   Naught shall make us rue
> If England to itself do rest but true.
> (*King John*, V,vii, 112–118)

London was the cultural, political, and social center of Elizabeth's
England. But in spite of its splendor and size in comparison with
other places in the nation, London was a medieval town, walled and
fortified. Aside from the royal palaces, most of the buildings were
commonplace, consisting chiefly of dwellings and shops. Outstand-

ing on the city's sky line were the Tower of London, St. Paul's Cathedral, and London Bridge.

Although much of the capital's trade and commerce depended on the court, government of the city itself lay in the hands of the twelve great livery companies. These organizations, descendants of medieval guilds, managed to elect the Lord Mayor, the aldermen, and the councilmen from their members. They made up the prosperous, conservative, stolid backbone of London's population. Also a part of this controlling group, much smaller in number than the guildsmen, were the professional men, of whom lawyers were the leaders. On the fringe were thousands of apprentices, many of whom came from respectable families and would ultimately achieve wealth and distinction in their chosen trades. At the bottom of the social ladder were the masses, poorly housed and fed, who led a hand-to-mouth existence. At the other extreme were the court and nobility; these ruled supreme in their palaces and on their estates but inspired little awe among London's independent middle class.

Open sewers and a prevailing absence of sanitation made the city far from pleasant. Writer after writer testified to the nauseating stench rising from streets and gutters. Still, London's population almost doubled during Elizabeth's reign. Harbage believes that in 1605 the total inhabitants of the metropolitan area approximated 160,000. Of these he estimates that 50,000 to 60,000 patronized the public theaters more or less regularly.[1]

Increasing wealth, extravagance, and luxury among the well-to-do classes permitted the introduction of many conveniences such as windows, forks, and toothpicks. Tobacco and expensive wardrobes became status symbols. Surplus spending money and leisure stimulated growth of the public stage; they likewise provoked Puritan disapproval.

Professor Harbage, who has also made a study of Elizabethan economy, states that in 1601 a master workman earned 16 pence per day, and an ordinary workman, about seven shillings (84 d.) per week. At this time one English penny had a purchasing power of approximately 31 cents today.

Any city needs entertainment outlets. London's consisted of taverns, brothels, animal-baiting pits, theaters, and miscellaneous attractions. A quart of sack cost eight pence; a quart of ale, four pence; a quart of weak beer, one penny. Tobacco was threepence a pipeload. Allusions to six-penny prostitutes suggest the cheapest rate in one of the more expensive diversions.

[1] See Alfred Harbage, *Shakespeare's Audience* (New York: Columbia University Press, 1941; reprinted, 1958), for a thorough review of the theater-goers of this period.

These prices are significant in showing the relative place of theaters in the entertainment and amusement world. One could purchase admission to a public theater (see p. 104) and standing room in the pit for one penny. For an additional penny a spectator could move into a gallery. For threepence a person could occupy the best seat in the Globe except for the shilling boxes bordering the stage itself. In contrast to these rates, the lowest admission to private theaters was sixpence.

This evidence makes it clear that Burbage, Henslowe, and their competitors catered to the masses of Londoners as well as to the middle and upper classes. The main stream of Elizabethan drama was entertainment on a popular level and not a special prerogative of prosperous businessmen and aristocrats.

Nor was this mixed audience so illiterate or uninformed as some critics have supposed. Various scholars have shown that most apprentices were able to read and write and probably had gone as far in formal education as Shakespeare himself had done. Certainly Shakespeare and his contemporaries gauged the capacity and taste of their audience, and available attendance figures indicate that they knew their trade. Drama written for the public playhouses was far superior in theatrical quality to that which the universities, law schools, guild halls, and private theaters produced.

This does not mean that Elizabethan Londoners were unanimous in their support of theaters. Some opposed drama for moral and religious reasons. Many more were apathetic. Elizabeth herself seems to have viewed the theater as a minor diversion and was less generous in her support of it than were many of her royal contemporaries. Nevertheless, playhouses were flourishing in 1603, when Elizabeth died and James I succeeded her. The new monarch gave enthusiastic encouragement to the stage and to playwrights, and attendance in public theaters continued in such a way as to make the period from 1558 through 1612 notable for the quantity and quality of its drama.

3. Elizabethan Drama and Stage before and during Shakespeare's Lifetime

During the first half of the sixteenth century a new and foreign-sprung dramatic force was making itself felt in England. Schoolmasters, seeking methods of increasing their students' interest and proficiency in Latin, began producing Roman plays in the schools.

Most popular of these were the comedies of Plautus and Terence and the tragedies of Seneca. The effect of this practice became clear when Nicholas Udall, a master at Eton and later at Westminster, wrote *Ralph Roister Doister* (1538–1553), a play which he based on Latin models and which scholars identify as the first "true" English comedy. A few years later gentlemen of the Inner Temple performed the first English tragedy, Thomas Norton's and Thomas Sackville's *Gorboduc*, as a part of their Christmas celebration in 1561/2. *Gorboduc* borrowed heavily from Senecan revenge tragedy and was also the first English play in blank verse.

Strolling Players

It was natural that professional companies of strolling players, whose offerings consisted of moralities and interludes, should start staging these new plays as they became available. Companies were eager to obtain dramatic material wherever they could get it, and their repertories began to reflect more of the "classical drama" which schoolmasters were encouraging. Dozens of new plays appeared between 1558 and 1580. That most of these possess little literary merit suggests the haste with which writers turned them out to meet increasing demands. In addition to professional adult companies, juvenile actors were giving performances at court and on private premises, as the nobility and the public became more avid in their support of drama.

In 1572 the government passed a famous statute in a long series of poor laws. Designed to remove shiftless and undesirable persons from streets, highways, and public places, and to provide for these persons' maintenance and support, the law listed strolling players along with vagabonds, bearwards, jugglers, and "sturdy beggars." Although the statute placed actors in the same category as these "near-criminal" classes, it also provided them with relief in the form of licensing through the sponsorship of a baron or peer of higher rank. The effect of this legislation was to bring players under the patronage of the nobility and ultimately under that of the Crown itself. One of the earliest of these licensed companies was the Earl of Leicester's Men. Subsequently this company joined with Lord Strange's Men to form the Lord Chamberlain's Company under the patronage of Henry Carey, Lord Hunsdon. Best-known of all Elizabethan troupes because Shakespeare was a member of it and because it gave notable performances in the Globe and Blackfriars theaters, this company became the King's Servants on May 19, 1603, after the accession of James I.

It was natural that players concentrated their activities in and around London, but influential forces steadfastly resisted and discouraged the acting of plays within the city's walls. Such opposition did not, however, check the growing popularity of drama among large numbers of citizens and especially among members of the peerage and court. As a result, London authorities had to content themselves with prohibiting performances on Sunday and with forbidding the erection of public playhouses inside the city. Some of this antagonism came from Puritan moral and religious objections to the theater, but most of it grew out of official zeal to maintain peace, reduce fire hazards, and control the plague.

Public Theaters

Consequently, when James Burbage built England's first public theater in 1576, he leased land from Giles Allen in the section of Shoreditch, which was outside the city proper. Burbage called his playhouse the Theatre. Best proof of its success was the erection, a few months afterward, of the Curtain in the same neighborhood.

Across London Bridge on the south bank of the Thames was the borough of Southwark. Within this district, bordering the river and extending westward from the bridge, was the area known as Bankside, notorious for its brothels, taverns, and bull-baiting and bearbaiting pits. Sometime between 1587 and 1592 Philip Henslowe erected the Rose theater there. About 1594 Francis Langley built the Swan farther to the west. These two theaters formed the nucleus of what was to become London's best-known Elizabethan theatrical district.

From 1597 to 1599 Richard and Cuthbert Burbage, sons of James, tried unsuccessfully to renew their lease with Giles Allen. Early in 1599 they removed the timbers of the Theatre and rebuilt their playhouse near the Rose and the Swan. They called it the Globe. Recognized as London's finest and best-equipped public theater, the Globe attracted faithful audiences until it caught fire and burned in 1613 during a performance of Shakespeare's *Henry VIII*. Powder charges from two cannon firing royal salutes settled on the thatched roof, and spectators and actors escaped with difficulty. The company rebuilt the Globe shortly after the disaster. In 1614 Henslowe erected the Hope in Bankside, but after some two years it became the scene of prize fights and animal baiting.

Elsewhere the Fortune and the Red Bull enjoyed public favor. Under the direction of Edward Alleyn and Philip Henslowe, the Fortune was the home of the Lord Admiral's Men, who maintained a spirited rivalry with the Globe and its company over a period of several years. The Red Bull catered to less sophisticated audiences and staged more sensational and melodramatic plays than those of its competitors. In time, most of the theaters were under the control and management of the Burbages (the Theatre, the Globe, and Blackfriars) or of Henslowe and Alleyn (The Rose, the Fortune, the Hope, and possibly the Swan).

Many students of the Elizabethan theater have attempted to reconstruct its physical appointments in great detail. Although individual houses may have differed in small ways and introduced added refinements and mechanical conveniences, it appears that the majority were very much alike. The playhouse itself was round or octagonal, with an open space or courtyard in the center. Spectators' galleries surrounded this yard on three levels. At the front and projecting into the yard was the stage itself. Behind the stage were dressing rooms, copy rooms (where the company kept its scripts), and space for properties and costumes.

Most scholars agree that the actual stage consisted of two parts: one was the inner stage, which was under roof and fitted with a curtain; the second was the outer, or apron, stage, which extended into the yard. In some of the later theaters, apparatus permitted performance on three different levels of the inner stage at heights corresponding to the spectators' galleries. Features of the apron stage included a large trapdoor near the center, smaller traps, and two pillars which supported a canopy ("the heavens") above the back part of the stage itself.[1]

From 1580 until 1642 there seems to have been an average of three to five playhouses operating simultaneously in London. Private theaters gave daily performances; public playhouses opened their doors as regularly as weather permitted. The cost of admission ranged from one penny to two and one-half shillings, depending on the location of the space. Some of the larger theaters apparently had a total capacity of approximately 2,500 people, almost one third of whom occupied the yard. Harbage estimates average attendance at the Rose at 1,250. The gross receipts for such a crowd amounted to about £8/9 (eight pounds, nine shillings).

Because of the location and facilities of public playhouses, performances took place in daylight, usually in the afternoon. Playwrights provided for the simulation of night and darkness by having characters carry candles or torches and by inserting appropriate lines in the dialogue. Writers also made frequent use of music, the or-

---

[1] Readers wishing to become more familiar with physical details of the Elizabethan theater should consult specialized works. Among these are: J. C. Adams, *The Globe Playhouse* (2nd ed.; New York: Barnes & Noble, Inc., 1961); Bernard Beckerman, *Shakespeare at the Globe* (New York: The Macmillan Company, 1962); C. Walter Hodges, *The Globe Restored* (Philadelphia: Albert Saifer, 1953); A. M. Nagler, *Shakespeare's Stage* (New Haven: Yale University Press, 1958); Irwin Smith, *Shakespeare's Globe Playhouse* (New York: Charles Scribner's Sons, 1957); Ashley H. Thorndike, *Shakespeare's Theater* (New York: The Macmillan Company, 1916, reprinted 1960).

chestra normally occupying the third or highest level of the inner stage. Costumes were elaborate and costly, the leading actors providing their own and possessing extensive wardrobes. Recent research suggests that sound effects and physical properties were in greater use than many people have supposed.

Playwrights

From this highly condensed review it is evident that by the 1580's organized companies playing in public theaters had created a demand for a constant supply of plays good enough to compete with London's other attractions. In many respects there was a "writers' market." Whereas these early playwrights received cash payments for their plays, their income from this source remained relatively modest. *Henslowe's Diary* [1] records sums paid to the twenty-odd writers who contributed plays to the Lord Admiral's Men from 1597 through 1603. Prices for plays ranged from £4 to £10/10, the usual payment being £6. Money then had perhaps twenty times the purchasing power that it has today, but Thomas Dekker, one of the most industrious playwrights of the era, probably earned the equivalent of no more than $3,000 in his busiest year. (During the reign of James I prices for plays were to increase, with the result that men of higher social quality and station were to write for the professional stage.)

Few writers became financially successful unless they enjoyed court favor or the patronage of wealthy devotees of literature or had additional income of some sort. The rare ones who acquired wealth combined the talents of acting and writing with sound business ability. Thomas Heywood acted for at least twenty-five years and wrote for forty. He was also a shareholder in one of the more popular companies. In 1633 he claimed to have had either "an entire hand, or at the least a main finger" in 220 plays. Like Heywood, Shakespeare was an actor. The Burbages granted him a full share in the Lord Chamberlain's Company, and he owned shares in both the Globe and Blackfriars theaters. Since there is no record of his having acted after 1603, most scholars assume that he devoted most of his time and talent to writing. In any event, his income, estimated at approximately $20,000 to $25,000 per annum (present-day value) during his later years, accrued chiefly from dividends from the company's profits rather than from direct payments for his thirty-seven plays.

Five playwrights emerged as the "giants" of the pre-Shakespearian

---

[1] *The Diary of Philip Henslowe* (see p. 104 above) gives valuable dates and other facts concerning the theaters he managed, the playwrights who wrote for him, and the expenses he incurred. The work is available in two editions: (1) ed. W. W. Greg, 1904–1908; (2) ed. R. A. Foakes and R. T. Rickert (New York: Cambridge University Press, 1961).

stage. Students of English drama designate them as the University Wits, a term which refers to their "brain power" rather than to their ability at making jokes or posing as college humorists. These five were John Lyly, George Peele, Robert Greene, Thomas Kyd, and Christopher Marlowe.[1] Although their lives overlapped with Shakespeare's, they began writing before he did and laid the framework of romantic comedy and tragedy which enabled their more illustrious successor to capture and dominate the Elizabethan stage.

First of the University Wits to gain public acclaim was John Lyly. Associated with the children of the Chapel Royal, Lyly devoted himself to writing chiefly for court audiences and for the Queen's favor. The great disappointment of his life was his failure to gain appointment as Master of the Revels, a lucrative court position. Famous for his artificial, elegant, balanced (euphuistic) prose, Lyly brought a consciousness and awareness of style and polish to English drama. Short-lived as the popularity of his writing was, he composed graceful lyrics and set a pattern which encouraged other playwrights to refine their own dramatic verse. Best-known of his plays is *Endymion;* another, *Campaspe,* contains the charming song which begins, "Cupid and my Campaspe played/At cards for kisses; Cupid paid."

George Peele was notable for his versatility. A competent poet, a patriotic Englishman, and an original and ingenious playwright, Peele experimented in pseudo-historical drama, pastoral comedy, and parody. In *The Arraignment of Paris* he adapted the classical story of Paris's awarding of the apple of Discord into a fulsome adulation of Queen Elizabeth. He was at his riotous best in *The Old Wives' Tale* with its blending of burlesque, folklore, and lyrics.

Robert Greene, dissolute and debauched, died at the age of thirty-five after he had gained first-hand acquaintance with the seamiest side of London's underworld. In spite of his dissipations Greene was a prolific writer and turned out an imposing number of pamphlets, narratives, descriptions of London life, and plays. Industrious as he was, Greene lived most of his short life in poverty.

Greene's most successful play was *Friar Bacon and Friar Bungay,* a combination of pastoral romanticism with white magic which set the pace for subsequent romantic comedies that were to eclipse it in reputation and quality. Consorting with prostitutes and the roughest cutthroats of his day, Greene nevertheless kept his plays singularly free of vulgarity. From his portrayal of female characters he won the title, "the Homer of women." Greene created every man's "ideal sweetheart"—the chaste, lively, attractive heroine—for the theater.

---

[1] Thomas Lodge and Thomas Nashe also belonged to this group of "Wits," but their most important literary contributions consisted of pamphlets, prose narratives, and non-dramatic poetry.

Intermittently irresponsible and repentant, he made his place as a talented writer despite his misfortunes.

Thomas Kyd's early life and career are equally obscure. It is uncertain whether or not he attended one of the universities, but his extant work places him with the other Wits in spirit. Kyd and Marlowe were friends, and both fell under government investigation for heresy. Put to torture, Kyd ascribed the authorship of an especially damaging anonymous pamphlet to Marlowe. He saved his neck, but he lost most of his friends and his own self-respect through his action. Kyd's claim to a place in English drama rests on *The Spanish Tragedy,* a play which enjoyed one of the longest and most sustained periods of popularity in the history of the English stage. Adapted from Senecan models, with many of Kyd's own innovations, this play was the prototype of a large number of Elizabethan revenge tragedies. Careful comparison between it and *Hamlet* shows some ten or twelve striking parallels in plot and characterization. Many critics ascribe an early, lost version of *Hamlet* to Kyd. Nevertheless, this playwright did not possess the poetic ability of his fellow Wits; his principal talents lay in contriving stage action and in manipulating plot and mechanics. *The Spanish Tragedy* contains few memorable lines, but neither does it have many dull or static scenes.

Last and most influential of the University Wits was Christopher Marlowe. Killed in a tavern brawl when he was twenty-nine, Marlowe left a group of tragedies which testify to his wide and deep reading and his independent thought. His major plays are: *Tamburlaine the Great* in two parts, *The Tragical History of Doctor Faustus, The Jew of Malta,* and *Edward II.* In *Tamburlaine* Marlowe presents the picture of a man obsessed with a craving for universal power and dominion; in *Faustus* the doctor seeks all knowledge; in *The Jew of Malta* Barabas desires controlling wealth; in *Edward II* the king is a tragic figure caught between an ambitious queen and peerage on one side and his personal favorites on the other. In all these plays Marlowe maintained an almost scholarly objectivity in dealing with his major characters and a freedom from expressing moral judgment and condemnation. Tamburlaine, "the scourge of God," dies a natural death, although his sadism and ruthlessness seem to merit both divine and poetic retribution. Faustus, alternately frightened and conscience-stricken by his pact with Lucifer, persists in his demoralizing contract and does not repent. Barabas, more avaricious and bloodthirsty than Shylock, proves as "honorable and trustworthy" as do the Christian Governor of Malta and Selim Calymath, the Moslem commander of the Turks. "Proud Mortimer" remains defiant to the very end of his life in *Edward II.* Plays like these, among the best dramatic offerings of their day, attracted audiences but did not win Marlowe many friends or admirers. He endured charges of blasphemy and heresy as well as vicious and unwarranted attacks on his personal and moral character.

Marlowe's early plays are one-man dramas. The title role dominates the action throughout. In *Edward II* he gave signs of developing a more balanced conflict among two or more major characters; this play is, in many ways, his best.

In style also, Marlowe set a new pace and established blank verse as the conventional vehicle for Elizabethan tragedy. He did not introduce this meter into English drama (see p. 103 above), but he developed and perfected it to the point where subsequent writers found it almost mandatory. His "mighty line" possessed a somewhat subtle and at times melodramatic quality. A student can find frequent evidences of Marlowe's influence on the plays of later authors; one example is *Richard III*, the most Marlovian of Shakespeare's plays.

Some of the University Wits were still writing after Shakespeare began his career. By the time he reached his full power as a playwright he was adapting many of their techniques and capitalizing on them, a fact which Robert Greene noted and criticized in a famous passage in *A Groatsworth of Wit Bought with a Million of Repentance*.[1] Many scholars find Shakespeare echoing Lyly's euphuistic style in *Love's Labour's Lost;* Peele's interest in historical drama is his series of chronicle plays; Greene's heroines and settings in *As You Like It* and *The Winter's Tale;* Kyd's blood and horror in *Titus Andronicus* and *Hamlet;* Marlowe's powerful lines in several of his tragedies. Certainly Shakespeare learned a great deal from the works of this group, and he benefited from their successes and shortcomings.

Nor was Shakespeare the only author to profit from this increasing interest in drama and demand for it. Thomas Dekker pleased London's craftsmen with his bourgeois comedy, *The Shoemakers' Holiday*. Ben Jonson became the acknowledged master of satirical comedy. Thomas Heywood wrote a notable domestic tragedy, *A Woman Killed with Kindness*. George Chapman, John Marston, Francis Beaumont, John Fletcher, Thomas Middleton, Philip Massinger—all wrote successful plays in the first half of the seventeenth century. John Webster won place next to Shakespeare as an author of tragedy with *The Duchess of Malfi*.

---

[1] In this pamphlet (1592) Greene advised three fellow playwrights to put no trust in actors, "for there is an upstart crow, beautified with our feathers, that with his *tiger's heart wrapped in a player's hide* supposes he is as well able to bombast out a blank verse as the best of you; and being an absolute *Johannes fac totum,* is in his own conceit the only Shake-scene in a country." The parody on York's description of Queen Margaret, "O tiger's heart wrapp'd in a woman's hide!" (*3 Henry VI*, I,iv, 137) and Shakespeare's name is obvious.

Printing of Plays

From the beginning, this activity on the stage created a growing demand for printed versions of plays, and London publishers were quick to take advantage of this new market. In the absence of copyright laws such as exist today, London printers banded themselves into the Royal Company of Stationers and maintained a *Register* for their mutual protection. By entering the title of any play, pamphlet, broadside, poem, or other item in this *Register* a printer or publisher could establish his rights to issue this particular work then or at some later date. There is ample evidence that most dramatic companies and producers, who owned the manuscripts of plays in their repertories, frequently made "staying entries" in the *Stationers' Register.*

Curiously, the purpose of these "staying entries" was not to provide for the printing of plays but to delay or prevent it altogether. Since there were no laws which reserved rights of production or royalties either to author or to producer, every company guarded its manuscripts with utmost care. Once a play appeared in print, any group of actors could purchase a copy and perform it. Scholars know that unprincipled actors, printers, or "promoters" printed several plays by Shakespeare and arranged for their unauthorized publication. Sometimes a company or author printed a second or "authentic" version in order to correct errors or corruptions in the pirated editions. It was also customary to publish plays after they had outlived their crowd-drawing appeal in the theater.

However effective or futile these attempts to protect publishers and printers may have been, the *Stationers' Register* provides a valuable record of authorship and date for a large number of Elizabethan plays. Whether an "entered" play appeared in print or not, it had to be in manuscript form at the time its owner officially listed it.

Since a large proportion of Elizabethan drama exists only in printed versions, some knowledge of printing practices is helpful in understanding many problems which arise concerning texts. This field of scholarship, known as bibliography, has become increasingly important in recent years.

Operating small hand presses, Elizabethan printers issued most of their books in one of three sizes. Presses at that time accommodated sheets of paper averaging twenty inches in length and fifteen inches in width. If a printer were preparing a large volume, he set his type so that he could print two pages on each side of a sheet. After the sheets passed through the press, workmen folded each one and gathered successive sheets together for sewing and binding.

If the printer folded these sheets of paper once, he created a *folio;* if he printed four pages on each side and folded each sheet twice, the result was a *quarto;* if he wanted a still smaller page, he increased the number of pages on each side of the sheet to eight and produced an *octavo.*

Because the quarto size was better suited to relatively short books, printers issued separate plays by Shakespeare in this form. But the John Heminge and Henry Condell collected edition of Shakespeare's plays in 1623 appeared in folio. Containing thirty-six of the thirty-seven plays commonly attributed to Shakespeare, this First Folio (there were three later folio editions) constitutes the one most important edition of his plays. Approximately half of these same plays appeared in one or more quarto editions before 1623; some of these were "bad quartos," others authorized ones.

Sound copies of the First Folio and of the various quartos are so expensive when they are available that only well-endowed libraries and wealthy collectors can purchase them, but most readers find a good modernized text of Shakespeare's works more satisfactory for studying purposes than are first editions or facsimiles of them. A conscientious editor uses original or facsimile copies of all of the extant early editions when he prepares a text. He compares the quartos (if any) with the folios. Usually there are many variations in spelling, punctuation, and frequently in the dialogue itself. To compile a good text, an editor must have an extensive historical knowledge of English, of printing practices and techniques, and of sixteenth-century literature, plus sound, objective common sense. Such skills require years of study and experience. The majority of readers must rely on the judgment of these experts who, like specialists in other highly technical fields, may disagree on details or on which one of several early editions holds the greatest authority.

Bibliographers explain many small variations in text as the products of conventions or errors in printing. Because their supply of type faces was limited, printers often had to set up the first and inside pages of a gathering,[1] run these through the press, and distribute the type before they could set the remaining pages in the same gathering. Microphotographic examination of individual letters proves that this happened. Printers faced another restriction when they came to "justify" their lines. The normal way in which to "justify" a line of type (that is, to make the beginning of the first word and the end of the last word flush with the page or column margins) is to insert small pieces of lead called quads between words in the line, thus pushing the last word to the margin. Elizabethan printers seem to have lacked an adequate supply of quads. They compensated for this by sticking in additional letters or removing

[1] After printing both sides of the paper, the printer folded the sheets to the required size and assembled them in small groups or collections for sewing and binding. Each assembly of sheets constituted a "gathering."

others where they did not confuse the identification of words. This probably explains how the same word can appear with two or three different spellings in as many lines. There was almost no standardization in spelling at this time, and printers felt freer to alter orthography than they would today.

These and other problems pose many questions for modern editors and students; such practices did not, of course, interfere to any great extent with the contemporary staging of plays. Playwrights and producers labored under other regulations and restrictions, however, some of which directly affected the language and subject matter of the dramas themselves.

Governmental Control

At the beginning of Elizabeth's reign a royal proclamation provided for the licensing of plays on a local level. Of greatest concern to the government was the suppression of sedition and heresy. City and county officials were probably lax and inconsistent in their performance of this duty. In 1574 the London Common Council, responding to increasing Puritan pressure, added a clause calling for control over "inchaste, uncomely, and unshamefaced speeches." Shortly before this the court had directed Leicester's Men to submit copies of plays to the Master of Revels for review and approval. In 1581 a royal patent enlarged and extended the powers of this official, in effect making him censor of the drama.

Originally appointed to arrange entertainment for the court, the Master of Revels gradually became responsible for the granting of permits to professional companies and for the licensing of plays for production. Edmund Tilney held the office from 1577 to 1610. Sir George Buc succeeded him and, with the backing of James I, expanded the duties of his position. Sir Henry Herbert purchased the Mastership for £150 a year in 1623 and became wealthy through collection of the various fees to which his licensing responsibilities entitled him. No wonder that John Lyly aspired to the office!

Always, subject matter suggesting sedition or heresy brought the swiftest and most energetic reaction from crown officials. One example of this type of censorship occurred when conspirators in the Essex uprising of 1601 arranged for a special revival of *Richard II* at the Globe. Queen Elizabeth immediately saw the comparison implied between Richard and herself. Shortly after the accession of James I, a passage in *Eastward Ho!* (1604) satirized Scots in a manner which roused the ire of the King and earned the authors, Jonson, Chapman, and Marston, a brief imprisonment in the Tower of London. Several plays incurred the displeasure and protest of foreign diplomats. In 1608 Chapman luckily escaped arrest when the

French ambassador complained vigorously about a production of *Biron's Conspiracy and Tragedy*. In 1624 Thomas Middleton's *A Game at Chess*, which Herbert had licensed for production, caustically attacked Count Gondomar, the recent Spanish ambassador. Official protests led to an order prohibiting the play's staging.

Direct legislation relating to hersey also occurred during the reign of James I. This was the so-called "Oath Act" of May 27, 1606, which prohibited the jesting or profane use of words designating God or persons of the Godhead on the stage. The parliamentary act prescribed a fine of ten pounds "for every such offence." Kenneth Muir believes that Macduff's words, ". . . if he scape,/Heaven forgive him too!" (IV,iii, 235) reflect a change from the actors' copy in order to conform to this law.[1]

In much the same fashion there were government regulations providing for the review, censorship, and licensing of books, plays, and other printed material. A royal *Injunction* of 1559 forbade the printing of any book or paper without the express written license of the Queen, or of six members of the Privy Council, or of certain high-ranking ecclesiastical officials. Even more important to the owners and publishers of plays was the Star Chamber *Decree* of June 23, 1586, which required the license of the Archbishop of Canterbury and Bishop of London (or their official deputies) for the "printynge of any booke, work, coppye, matter, or any other thinge" (E. K. Chambers, *The Elizabethan Stage,* III, 161–168, and IV, 303). In 1607 responsibility for correcting and approving plays passed to the office of the Master of Revels.

Another factor which often curtailed the activities of professional companies was the plague. Usually, when ravages of the disease were heavy, the Mayor and Aldermen of London appealed to the Privy Council to ban plays. When incidence of the plague decreased, the Council commanded the city to permit the reopening of certain private theaters. In 1593 the Council prohibited plays in London or within seven miles of it. Similar but less drastic restrictions obtained in 1594. In 1603, 1604, 1619, and 1625, the closing of theaters seems to have depended on the total deaths per week in the city. The crucial number varied from thirty to fifty.

In summary, official controls of drama during the Elizabethan and Stuart periods fall into three categories. The throne concerned itself with seditious and heretical material and with objectionable attacks on foreign powers. City authorities sought to maintain peace and order and frowned on immoral and scandalous subject matter and speech. All levels of government recognized the necessity of quarantine measures in time of plague.

---

[1] See *Macbeth,* ed. Kenneth Muir, note on IV,iii, 235 (p. 140).

4. William Shakespeare

Many books have assembled facts, reasonable suppositions, traditions, and speculations concerning the life and career of William Shakespeare.[1] Taken as a whole these materials give a rather comprehensive picture of England's foremost dramatic poet. Tradition and sober supposition are not necessarily false because they lack proved bases for their existence. It is important, however, that persons interested in Shakespeare should distinguish between *facts* and *beliefs* about his life.

Shakespeare the Man

From one point of view modern scholars are fortunate to know as much as they do about a man of middle-class origin who left a small country town and embarked on a professional career in sixteenth-century London. From another point of view they know surprisingly little about the writer who has continued to influence the English language and its drama and poetry for more than three hundred years. Sparse and scattered as these facts of his life are, they are sufficient to prove that a man from Stratford by the name of William Shakespeare wrote the major portion of the thirty-seven plays which scholars ascribe to him. The concise review which follows will concern itself with some of these records.

No one knows the exact date of William Shakespeare's birth. His baptism occurred on Wednesday, April 26, 1564.[2] His father was John Shakespeare, tanner, glover, dealer in grain, and town official

---

[1] Among the best are J. Q. Adams, *A Life of William Shakespeare* (New York: Houghton Mifflin Co., 1923), a definitive biography; G. E. Bentley, *Shakespeare: A Biographical Handbook* (New Haven: Yale University Press, 1961), sound and up to date; E. K. Chambers, *William Shakespeare* (2 vols., New York: Oxford University Press, 1930), the collected opinions of one of England's most distinguished Elizabethan scholars; M. G. Chute, *Shakespeare of London* (New York: E. P. Dutton & Co., 1949), readable and generally accurate, but does not always distinguish carefully between fact and opinion; Edward Dowden, *Shakspere, a Critical Study of His Mind and Art* (New York: Harper & Brothers, 1873; reprinted, 1962), dated but influential on later criticism and still useful; J. Dover Wilson, *The Essential Shakespeare* (New York: Cambridge University Press, 1932), a lively and entertaining treatment by a brilliant and provocative critic and editor.

[2] A tradition exists that William Shakespeare died on the same day of the month as that on which he was born. This, together with a study of contemporary practice in christening infants, has led most biographers to suggest that his birthday was April 23.

of Stratford; his mother, Mary, was the daughter of Robert Arden, a prosperous gentleman-farmer. The Shakespeares lived on Henley Street.

Under a bond dated November 28, 1582, William Shakespeare and Anne Hathaway entered a marriage contract. The baptism of their eldest child, Susanna, took place in Stratford in May, 1583. One year and nine months later their twins, Hamnet and Judith, were christened in the same church. The parents named them for the poet's friends, Hamnet and Judith Sadler.

Early in 1596 William Shakespeare, in his father's name, applied to the College of Heralds for a coat of arms. Although positive proof is lacking, there is reason to believe that the Heralds granted this request, for in 1599 William again made application for the right to quarter his coat of arms with that of his mother. Entitled to her father's coat of arms, Mary had lost this privilege when she had married John Shakespeare before he held the official status of gentleman; approval by the Heralds of the request of 1596 would have restored this distinction to her.

In May of 1597 William purchased New Place, the outstanding residential property in Stratford at that time. Since John Shakespeare had suffered financial reverses prior to this date, William must have achieved success for himself.

Court records show that in 1601–1602 William Shakespeare began rooming with the household of Christopher Mountjoy in London. Subsequent disputes over the wedding settlement and agreement between Mountjoy and his son-in-law, Stephen Belott, led to a series of legal actions. In 1612 the court scribe recorded Shakespeare's deposition of testimony relating to the case.

In July, 1605, William Shakespeare paid £440 for the lease of a large portion of the tithes [1] on certain real estate in and near Stratford. This was possibly the most important and successful investment of his lifetime, and it paid a steady income for many years.

John Combe, resident of Stratford, died on July 12, 1614. To his friend William Shakespeare he bequeathed the sum of £5. These records and similar ones are important, not because of their economic significance but because they prove the existence and activity of the man William Shakespeare in Stratford and London during this period.

On March 25, 1616, William Shakespeare revised his last will and

---

[1] This was an arrangement whereby Shakespeare purchased half the annual tithes, or taxes, on certain agricultural products from parcels of land in and near Stratford. In addition to receiving approximately 10 per cent income on his investment, he almost doubled his capital.

testament. He died on April 23 of the same year. His body lies within the chancel and before the altar of the Stratford church.

> Good Frend for Iesvs sake forbeare,
> To digg the dvst encloased heare;
> Bleste be ẙ man ẙ spares thes stones,
> And cvrst be he ẙ moves my bones.

Hamnet died in 1596, John Shakespeare in 1601, Mary Shakespeare in 1608. Surviving William were his wife Anne, who died August 6, 1623; Susanna, wife of Dr. John Hall; and Judith, wife of Thomas Quiney. The last direct descendant of William Shakespeare was his granddaughter, Elizabeth Hall, who married Thomas Nash.

These are the most outstanding facts about Shakespeare the man as apart from those about the dramatist and poet. Such pieces of information, scattered from 1564 through 1616, declare the existence of such a person, not as a writer or actor, but as a private citizen. It is illogical to think that anyone would or could have fabricated these details for the purpose of deceiving later generations.

Shakespeare the Actor and the Playwright

In similar fashion, the evidence establishing William Shakespeare as the foremost playwright of his day is positive and persuasive. Robert Greene's *Groatsworth of Wit* (see p. 115), in which he attacked Shakespeare, a mere actor, for presuming to write plays in competition with Greene and his fellow playwrights, was entered in the *Stationers' Register* on September 20, 1592. In 1594 Shakespeare acted before Queen Elizabeth, and in 1594/95 his name appeared as one of the shareholders of the Lord Chamberlain's Company.

Francis Meres in *Palladis Tamia* (1598) called Shakespeare "mellifluous and hony-tongued" and compared his comedies and tragedies with those of Plautus and Seneca in excellence. Meres listed twelve plays Shakespeare had written, eleven of which are extant.[1]

Shakespeare's continued association with Burbage's company is equally definite. His name appears as one of the owners of the Globe in 1599. On May 19, 1603, he and his fellow actors received a patent from James I designating them as the King's Men and making them Grooms of the Chamber. Late in 1608 or early in 1609, Shakespeare and his colleagues purchased the Blackfriars Theatre and began

---

[1] Meres mentioned *Love's Labour's Won*. Despite attempts by many scholars to identify this play under a variant title, there is no certain proof that it has survived.

using it as their winter location when weather made production at the Globe inconvenient.

Other specific allusions to Shakespeare, to his acting and his writing, occur in numerous places. Put together they form irrefutable testimony that William Shakespeare of Stratford and London was the leader among Elizabethan playwrights.

One of the most impressive of all proofs of Shakespeare's authorship of his plays is the First Folio of 1623, with the dedicatory verse which appeared in it. John Heminge and Henry Condell, members of Shakespeare's own company, stated that they collected and issued the plays as a memorial to their fellow actor. Many contemporary poets contributed eulogies to Shakespeare as author. One of the best-known of these poems is by Ben Jonson, one-time fellow actor and later a friendly rival. Jonson also criticized Shakespeare's dramatic work in *Timber: or, Discoveries* (printed 1641).

Certainly there are many things about Shakespeare's genius and career which the most diligent scholars do not know and cannot explain, but the *facts* which do exist are sufficient to establish Shakespeare's identity as a man and his authorship of the thirty-seven plays which reputable critics acknowledge to be his.

Writers who have attempted to deny that Shakespeare was a historical figure or that he wrote these plays and have tried to show that some other individual was their creator overlook or ignore the basic facts which are available to them. Alleged cryptograms and codes which claim authorship for someone else break down when expert cryptographers test them. Arguments for such people as Francis Bacon, Chrisopher Marlowe, the Earl of Oxford, and others present more difficulties when one examines them than does the modest list of facts supporting William Shakespeare. Someone obviously wrote these dramatic masterpieces, and Shakespeare remains the only candidate worthy of serious consideration.[1]

5. Chronology of Shakespeare's Plays

Differences of opinion exist concerning the dates when Shakespeare wrote his plays. A working order is, nevertheless, helpful, and

[1] For a recent and detailed discussion of this controversy the reader should consult H. N. Gibson, *The Shakespeare Claimants* (New York: Barnes & Noble, Inc., 1962).

the following sequence, with a slight overlapping of periods, represents a consensus of leading editors.

Dates	Comedies	Histories	Tragedies
1589–1595	*Love's Labour's Lost* *Comedy of Errors* *Two Gentlemen of Verona* *Midsummer Night's Dream*	*1, 2, 3 Henry VI* *Richard III* *King John*	*Titus Andronicus* *Romeo and Juliet*
1595–1603	*Merchant of Venice* *Taming of the Shrew* [1] *Much Ado About Nothing* *Merry Wives of Windsor* *As You Like It* *Twelfth Night*	*Richard II* *1, 2 Henry IV* *Henry V*	*Julius Caesar*
1601–1609	*Troilus and Cressida* [2] *All's Well That Ends Well* *Measure for Measure* *Pericles*		*Hamlet* *Othello* *King Lear* *MACBETH* *Antony and Cleopatra* *Timon of Athens* *Coriolanus*
1609–1613	*Cymbeline* *Winter's Tale* *Tempest*	*Henry VIII*	

[1] Some editors believe that *The Taming of the Shrew* appeared as early as 1594.

[2] Scholars have differed in their classification of *Troilus and Cressida*. In the First Folio it stands between the Histories and the Tragedies. Today the majority of critics treat it as a comedy.

INDEX

123